Worth
the
Cost?

Worth the Cost?

Becoming a Doctor
Without Forfeiting Your Soul

by Jack Tsai, MD

Healthy Life Press
Orlando, Florida

WORTH THE COST?

©2013 by Jack Tsai, MD
All Rights Reserved.

Published by:

Healthy Life Press • 2603 Drake Drive • Orlando, FL 32810
www.healthylifepress.com

Cover and Internal Designs: Judy Johnson
Cover Photos: Laurie Au
Printed in the United States of America

Library of Congress Cataloging-in-Publication Data
Tsai, Jack, MD
    Worth the Cost?

ISBN 978-1-939267-71-9
1. Christian Life – Discipleship;
2. Christian Doctors – Personal Growth

Undesignated Scripture references are taken from THE HOLY BIBLE, NEW INTERNATIONAL VERSION®, Copyright© 1973, 1978, 1984 by the International Bible Society. One quotation is from the New American Standard Bible, Copyright© 1960, 1962, 1963, 1968, 1971, 1972, 1973, 1975, 1977 by the Lockman Foundation. Used by permission. All rights reserved worldwide.

The opinions expressed in this book are solely the author's and they do not necessarily reflect the perspective of any organization that is mentioned in the book, or with which he is now or has ever been associated.

To Priscilla,
who lovingly puts up with all my shenanigans,

And to God,
who continues to pour out grace undeserving.

Contents

Preface

I DON'T USUALLY LIKE TO TALK ABOUT MYSELF, AND I ESPE-cially don't like to so obviously brag about past accomplishments, being the good Asian that I am. And even worse is bragging to people who don't know me. But at the risk of sounding conceited, I have to say that growing up I was the model Asian boy. If there were some sort of Asian poster Gerber baby and I were better looking, it would be me.

I was one of those kids who loved to be good. You know, obedient, didn't talk to strangers, and did well in school. My music instrument of choice? The violin. (This is a requirement of being Asian; piano and maybe the flute are acceptable choices, too.) I performed in all the orchestra concerts, recitals, and competitions. My parents fortunately allowed me to participate in sports, so I played tennis (surprise!) throughout high school.

And I didn't mind school so much. Test-taking was actually enjoyable. Literally, I felt a sense of joy filling in

Scantron bubbles. (Yes, I'm sick. I have asthma.) I probably wasn't as ambitious as I could have been when it came to picking colleges. Proximity to home was important, so I applied mostly to a handful of schools in California.

The decision came down to UC Berkeley or UCLA, and UCLA won out because it was closer. Since I was quite the mama's boy (still am!), I wanted to be able to visit often. I ended up coming home almost every weekend throughout college. And the grand finale? I eventually got into medical school, fulfilling every Asian parent's dream.

Up until that point, I did everything right in the eyes of my parents, and in the eyes of the world. I was on my way to what many would consider a successful and secure future, to obtaining the American Dream . . . until I decided to take seriously God's command to die to myself and follow in obedience after Jesus.

Although I became a Christian in high school, my personal plans did not come in conflict with God's call to discipleship with Jesus until I was in medical school. Choosing God's will over my own ambitions, I ended up in one of the least respected fields of medicine as my specialty in order to serve the uninsured. After finishing my training, I decided to work part-time (making even less), enrolled in seminary (actually paying money), and got more involved in church ministry (not being paid at all).

What's this book about?

This book is about that journey and what I learned about the values of this world, the state of healthcare, and what it really means to be a follower of Jesus Christ. It is a reflection on my medical training, what I had hoped to gain, and the hidden costs I discovered along the way. This road will demand of you not just your money and peak years of life. If you let it, it can consume your soul.

Many well-meaning Christians wanting to use medicine for God's glory are side-tracked somewhere along the way because of the academic pressure, the false promises of this world, and the spiritual and emotional burn-out, just to list a few pitfalls. If you are thinking about embarking on this journey, the big question for you to consider is first, is this all worth it? Then, if you still wish to proceed, you have to think through how to avoid neglecting your soul in the process. I present in this book answers I have found helpful.

What this book isn't about is how to get into medical school, although I threw in some pearls along the way. There are plenty of resources out there about all the gory details of the entire application process. Rather, this book is a guide on how to think about making a decision to pursue medicine (or any career for that matter), and how to integrate your relationship with God into that decision.

If you join me in this adventure, you might laugh, maybe cry, but probably not. My hope, though, is that in reading, you will pray. And not just pray, "God, please get me into medical school." Pray that our God, who desires that we partner alongside Him in His salvation plan, would give us wisdom and courage to choose His will over our own. If we had more robust prayer lives, we probably wouldn't need books like this. But that's not good advertisement, so pretend I didn't say that.

In Part I, we will explore some major reality checks I experienced going through the medical training process. It definitely wasn't all puppies and rainbows. Hopefully it will help you think through your motives for pursuing medicine and weigh the costs involved. Before you make the decision to become a physician, life has some bigger questions you have to answer first, particularly about God and what He has to say about His Son, Jesus.

If you feel God calling you into medicine (or any other field), Part II will address the question, "What now?" Figuring out God's calling for your life is one thing. Actually carrying it out is another thing altogether. What do we need to do to prepare so that when we are actually on the other end, ready to do God's work in whatever field, we still want to? How can our faith not just survive as we endure the rigors of training, but thrive as we grow deeper in relationship with God and in our understanding of His heart?

Lastly, Part III offers some final thoughts and words of encouragement to embrace the calling God has for you, rather than unintentionally (or intentionally) settling for a life chasing after empty promises. This world offers plenty of those. I've included reflection questions at the end of each chapter intended to help you think through how God is working in your life.

Who should read this book?

When I started this project, I had in mind mainly those wanting to jump on the medical bandwagon, or who are in the middle of applying. But a big question I want to address is how we can keep God's convictions throughout our training so we will actually carry them out when we finally have the skills. If you are well into your training, this is important for you to consider. So, whether you are just thinking about applying or paying off your medical school loans, my completely unbiased recommendation is that you should read this book.

And just so I don't get in trouble for false advertising, this book ultimately is about Christian discipleship, what it means to follow after Christ. As much as I want success in your professional endeavors, I care much more about your relationship with your Creator God. Even if you are not interested in medicine, you can replace "doctor" in the sub-title with your career of choice and these truths can still apply. I'm simply using the medical career as an extreme case study to point out principles for Christian living and stumbling blocks that can trip anyone up as you seek to carry out God's will.

Having made that disclosure, if you are not a Christian and could care less about Jesus, don't throw this book away just yet.[1] Perhaps God is using this opportunity to draw you closer to Him. What do you have to lose? Chances are someone bought this for you. Even if you did buy this not realizing it was actually a "Christian" book, you already paid for it so you might as well read it. It might take away a few hours of your life. Not a bad investment, though, if it helps you figure out where you will be spending the rest of eternity.

Parents should read this, especially Christian parents. Chapter 9 is specifically for you. Unfortunately, a big barrier to Christian obedience is well-meaning Christian parents who understandably want the best for their kids, but are confused about the meaning of "best." To all the tiger moms and dragon dads out there, please don't get mad at me if your kid doesn't end up going to medical school.

I suppose if you are just bored, you can read this as well. Or if you are my friend, I will be personally offended if you didn't read this and buy three copies to give to your friends. At least.

Introduction: My Story

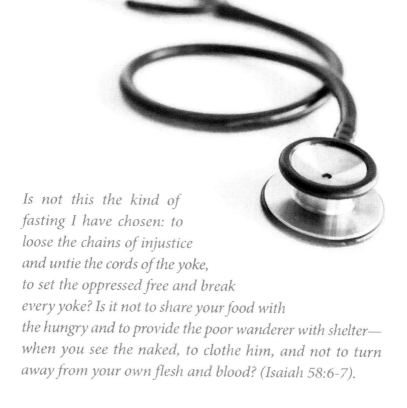

Is not this the kind of
fasting I have chosen: to
loose the chains of injustice
and untie the cords of the yoke,
to set the oppressed free and break
every yoke? Is it not to share your food with
the hungry and to provide the poor wanderer with shelter—
when you see the naked, to clothe him, and not to turn
away from your own flesh and blood? (Isaiah 58:6-7).

Calling

I WAS AT THE ANNUAL AMERICAN ACADEMY OF FAMILY Physicians conference in 2011. I had just finished my residency training and had decided to stay on to do a faculty development fellowship to see if academia was something I wanted to pursue. Our department was at the conference recruiting and amidst that celebration of primary care, I reflected a bit on my own personal journey as a physician and how I had ended up in this field.

At that time family medicine looked like a great choice, with primary care at the center of healthcare reform and all the buzz about Patient-Centered Medical Homes. It certainly was (and still is) an exciting time to be in primary care. But four years prior to that, making that decision as a fourth year medical student was more a step of faith, not in the future trend of medicine, but in what I thought was God's calling.

To be honest, right up until the fourth year of medical school, I never thought about family medicine. Actually, I did have thoughts, but they were pretty negative. Wasn't family medicine for those who weren't smart enough to get into the specialty fields? After all, it is among the lowest paying fields, why would anyone choose that voluntarily?

And my scores were good enough. I didn't study my butt off and love filling in Scantron bubbles for nothing. So it came as quite a shock to many when I made my decision. It particularly shocked my dad, being an anesthesiologist with many specialist friends whose kids were in medical school becoming specialists as well. During that time, it was like playing specialty roulette with him trying to sell me a different medical career each time we spoke, wanting to change my mind.

So why did I choose family medicine? Well, first off, in addition to being a large academic center, my medical school operated a great system of student-run free clinics (much kudos to the many physicians who dedicated their careers to serve the uninsured of San Diego). It was through my involvement there, specifically through the street outreach van, that I was first exposed to the great need for primary care. We would drive all around downtown San Diego offering basic services, trying to connect the homeless to care. During this time my faith finally began to intersect with my professional life.

I had known I wanted to become a doctor way before I became a Christian in high school. Like I mentioned, my dad is an anesthesiologist and my mom was a nurse. Add bad asthma, frequent doctor visits, and a sprinkle of hospitalizations to the pot and you get a neurotic, determined pre-med as a result. It also helped that I liked science and had at least the bare minimum of social skills.

After I accepted Christ, nothing really changed in that regard. I went happily off to college, majored in physiological science like a good little pre-med, and researched and volunteered my way into medical school. In medical school, I just looked for Christian things that I should do. So, I started volunteering at the free clinics, as well as going down to Mexico on weekend mission trips. I was a medical student who happened to be a Christian.

Then I met Dr. Nick Yphantides, a mentor who would change the trajectory of my medical career. Growing up, my heroes were Jackie Chan and my dad, and I quickly added Dr. Nick to that list. He was one of those superstar students who made medical school look like child's play. He graduated high school and college early, and rumor has it he got top marks in every class and rotation in medical school.

This was a guy who could have done anything he wanted. But he was also a devoted Christian who loved the Lord, and was convicted by God to serve the indigent poor of San Diego. Because of that, he chose to go into primary care and spent the first decade of his career on the front lines serving exclusively patients without insurance.

In Dr. Nick I found a Christian who happened to be a doctor. He understood that God's heart beats for the poor,

oppressed, and marginalized. For Dr. Nick, medicine was
simply a means in which to carry out that heart. As I spent
time with him and saw that passion lived out, God began
to put a similar conviction on my heart as well.[2]

Alongside these experiences, the Bible began to speak
to me, opening my eyes to God's desire for His people to
care not just for the spiritually lost, but for the physically
hurt as well. Passages like
Matthew 25:31-46 about
the sheep and the goats,
and Isaiah 58 about true
religious acts express very
clearly God's heart for
those who are suffering
physically, and for true believers to do something
about it. One of the signs
proving Jesus was the Messiah was He healed the sick, giving us a hint that physical health matters in God's kingdom.

> I was on my way
> to obtaining the
> American Dream . . .
> until I decided to
> take seriously
> God's command
> to die to myself.

God challenged me to use medicine to carry out His
heart for justice and mercy and, as I looked at the mess
that is our healthcare system, there was plenty to do. I did-
n't understand all the politics involved at the time (and I
still don't really), but I knew there were too many people
suffering from complications of completely preventable
diseases because of either a lack of insurance, or a lack of
access to care, even with insurance.

As I am writing this, almost fifty million Americans are
without health insurance. And it isn't just poor people. I
was denied coverage because of my asthma, a pre-existing

condition, and ended up with a thousand dollar-plus emergency room bill because I ran out of my maintenance inhalers. Even if we got a total revamp of our healthcare system expanding coverage, there will always be people without adequate access to primary care services.

And so for me, God put on my heart to use medicine to tangibly and practically obey that command to love those who are in need. While every medical field seeks to alleviate suffering, family medicine seemed like the obvious choice to provide the most basic care to those who needed it the most.

But it was not an easy choice. As much as we want to say money doesn't matter, a hundred thousand dollar per year salary differential in some cases really does a number on your personal convictions. On top of that, my dad is one of the biggest role models in my life, and to know that I chose something with which he didn't agree was heart wrenching. It also didn't help that there were attendings in other specialties who quite openly put down family medicine.

As the promises of wealth and prestige tugged at my heart, I had to come back to the truth that Jesus is the Lord of my life, not me. I will go into more details in Chapter 1, but I had to remind myself that following Christ meant not just believing in Jesus for the forgiveness of sins to get into heaven, but being willing to obey whatever God was calling me to. God had been faithful in bringing me this far; I could continue to trust in Him to step out in faith. By God's grace and strength, I was able to follow through with my convictions.

Of course this is not to say that as a Christian you can't be a radiologist, dermatologist, or whatever other specialty. By no means! There is a great need for Christians in every field, and God's kingdom can be advanced whatever your specialty. But for me, to have chosen another field would have been disobedient to what I felt God calling me to. Subsequently, I chose the family medicine program at Harbor-UCLA because its mission statement aligned very nicely with mine: To train physicians to serve the medically underserved.

New Beginnings

My residency training was an amazing experience. There really isn't a better place to train than at a county facility in my opinion. As a testament to the program's dedication to raising up physicians to work with the underserved, I'm happy to say that at the end of my time there, I still came out with the same convictions I had going into residency.

It wasn't all roses and sunshine, though. Many times I doubted my decision to go into family medicine and, in particular, to care for the underserved. It didn't take too long for my grand scheme of changing the world through the love of Christ in healthcare to run up against some harsh realities. Some days I wished I could go back to memorizing the Kreb cycle. It was going to take the support of my church community, fellow Christians in medicine, and my personal relationship with God to keep me on the path of His calling. I will unpack more of this wrestling throughout the book.

At the end of my residency, I decided to stay on for an extra year as chief and a faculty development fellow to explore academic medicine. To make a long story short, I discovered that I really enjoy teaching and working with the residents. I also saw how being in academics could be strategic in improving care for the underserved through research on care delivery. I even started the application process for becoming a faculty member, but at the end of that year, I decided to put that on hold as I felt God pulling me in yet another unexpected direction.

To be honest, when I was searching the job market near the end of my training, I had to again make the conscious decision to die to my own desires and ambitions. Even within family medicine there is a large salary discrepancy between private and federally funded community clinics. I remember sitting in on one job presentation by a large private organization, and it was so, so attractive. I could make almost forty percent more working for them compared to what the community clinics offered, and that was not even including the bonuses and other benefits. Suddenly, all these thoughts crossed my mind:

Did God really call you to work with the poor?
Just do some volunteering when you have free time.
Think about how much money you can donate.

Now, some of those thoughts weren't necessarily bad. Sure you can do more ministry with more money. And obviously it's not a sin to work for a private organization. But for me, again, I knew I would be betraying the conviction of providing care for the underserved that God had placed on my heart if I had pursued that job. So, I took a position in a community clinic organization serving the medically underserved of Long Beach working in their various sites, including their homeless clinic. I did stay on as staff in my residency program on a per diem basis doing some teaching to keep my foot in academics. And actually, between the two jobs, I decided to work only part-time.

Oh, by the way, at the end of residency in May of 2011, I got married to Priscilla, the girl of my dreams! I really did dream about her, and in both instances I told her I liked her and she rejected me. That story is in another book in the works (maybe).

One important aspect of our relationship is our involvement at South Bay Evangelical Christian Church, the same church in which I was saved back in high school.[3] I was involved in church activities throughout college, coming back almost every weekend to serve (and to see my mom). Being away for medical school was hard, but I was able to plug into ministry when I moved back for residency. Eventually I joined the leadership team and took on more responsibilities, including teaching and preaching.

During this time of figuring out our future direction, Priscilla and I were also praying about our involvement at church. Even though ministry was not on either of our radars while we were growing up, God was doing some funny things in arranging circumstances so that slowly we were getting more and more involved in church work. Since I was speaking from the pulpit (more like a music stand), I wanted to take some seminary classes to help me do that more effectively (and to avoid teaching heresy).

But with full-time work, our present church involvement, and recently being married, we were already having a hard time balancing the commitments we had.

After much praying and talking with some of the elders, Priscilla and I decided (admittedly with some reluctance) that ministry was something God had gifted us for and in which He was calling us to become more involved. We agreed I would work part-time in order to have time and energy to take some classes and assume more responsibilities at church. We committed our plan to God and He worked out the details, providing a part-time position with flexible hours, and opening the doors to seminary. I started classes at Talbot School of Theology in the fall of 2012.

> As the promises of wealth and prestige tugged at my heart, I had to come back to the truth that Jesus is the Lord of my life.

Priscilla also started looking for a job that would allow her to be at church consistently and be available for our different summer activities. Previously she was doing in-patient medicine, working the 3 p.m.-11 p.m. shift and every other weekend. (Did I mention she's a nurse?) That schedule precluded her from regular church attendance, and the work was emotionally and physically exhausting, leaving her little to invest in ministry. Not too long after we made the decision, God provided a school nurse position that not only freed up her weekends and summers, but was more in line with Priscilla's heart to do public health. That was a huge answer to prayer, undoubtedly God's sovereign hand at work as the other nurses interviewing seemed more qualified and experienced. This provision served as an additional confirmation that this was the right decision to make.

Still, this wasn't an easy decision, and was actually scarier than choosing to go into family medicine. When we met with our church elder who supervises the English ministry, he said something along the lines of, "If you pursue ministry, the only promise I can make is you will experience heartbreak and suffering." Not that he was jaded and burnt out from church service, but he understood how difficult providing soul care is. This is another career that shouldn't be entered into lightly. (Perhaps someone should write a book about this too!) And even with our limited church involvement thus far we had experienced to a small extent what Paul said in 2 Corinthians 11:28, "Besides everything else, I face daily the pressure of my concern for all the churches."

But we had also experienced the joys and fruits of ministry. I'm scared to even think about how I would have turned out without my church investing in me, and I saw how God was using this ministry to shape and impact the next generation. And so, despite our many fears and doubts, we decided to take a step forward knowing that we couldn't see ourselves not involved in church ministry.

You can imagine my parents were not big fans of this decision. My dad had all these plans for me after residency, now that I had become a real doctor supposedly making real doctor money. He wanted us to buy a house with him so we could get more tax deductions, start a college fund for our unborn children, and implement many other wealth-building strategies. Not that he's a greedy person, but he wanted to make sure his son was taken care of, and I appreciate him for that. But for me it was such a striking contrast between building up God's kingdom versus spending all my energy trying to build up my own "kingdom."

Now, for all the fun I poke at the stereotypical Asian parents, I have to say my parents have been unexpectedly supportive. They are not believers, but once they realized my faith was genuine and not just a phase, they gave me the freedom to pursue it. I love my parents and appreciate all they have done for me. If they had not helped majorly with my school debt, I wouldn't be as free to serve the Lord. But without Christ, my post-medical school decisions have been foolishness, not just in the eyes of the world, but in their eyes as well.

After all, in the world's thinking, why would you go into one of the lowest paying fields in the first place? Why would you then take on a lower paying position, work less hours so that you are making even less, and on top of that pay tuition to do something you aren't being paid to do? Why would you put your career on hold for something that's not going to do anything for you professionally in the future?

As I write this, I'm involved in patient care of the underserved, teaching residents, attending seminary, and preaching at my church. It definitely is not at all what I had envisioned when I entered medical school, and it might seem like I'm a bit confused in terms of my purpose in life. And maybe I am. But if you think about it, isn't this similar to what Jesus went around doing? Matthew 4:23 says, "Jesus went throughout Galilee, teaching in their synagogues, preaching the good news of the kingdom, and healing every disease and sickness among the people." I just want to be like Jesus.

*   *   *

I am not sure what the future will look like, especially if little Jacks and Priscillas come into the picture. At the rate I'm taking classes, it will take me six years to finish this two-year seminary MA program. Maybe I'll only be able to take one or two years of classes and have to call it quits. Perhaps I'll love it so much I'll take ten years and get the full Master of Divinity degree. Maybe God will grow our church and I'll end up in full-time ministry. Or maybe the ministry will fizzle out and I'll focus mostly on patient care, who knows. I'm not very used to living with such uncertainty, but there has been such an intimacy with God that I haven't experienced in a long while.

One of the first classes I took at Talbot inspired me to write this book. I was challenged to pray about the unique experiences God had brought me through, and in particular my journey in medicine thus far, and how I can integrate my faith to help others navigate their choices in obedience to the Scriptures and the leading of the Holy Spirit. What started as a reflection project turned into a book idea, and somehow miraculously turned into a book. So I do not write this because I am an expert, or even consider myself an author. This is all a result of the promptings of the Holy Spirit and God's grace in my life.

To all the parents who have asked me to talk to their kids and to the equally neurotic, determined pre-med students who wonder if they should pursue medicine, I offer this book. It is a compilation of my personal experiences, previous reflections in my blog and sermons, and my interactions with others on the medical path. If you are thinking this is too much to read, don't worry, it's not a very long book. But if you aren't willing to put in some work, then you, my friend, should probably not pursue the eleven-plus post-high school years that is the journey of medicine. And that's just the training.

I had very different ideas of medicine way back before embarking on this journey. I wish I had spent more time learning about and preparing for the realities of medical practice, and the hardship of medical training. Instead of asking, "How do I get into medical school?" you ought to figure out first if you really want to get there.

Reflection Questions

1. What are some key influences that have shaped your life (e.g., relocations, special relationships, tragic events, and personal trials)? How did these people/events help to clarify or redirect your steps?

2. How did you become interested in medicine (or any career)? List all your motivations for wanting to go into this field.

3. If you are a Christian, remind yourself of how you came to put your faith in Christ. Have your future aspirations ever conflicted with God's call to discipleship?

Part I
Are You Sure You Want to Go to Medical School?

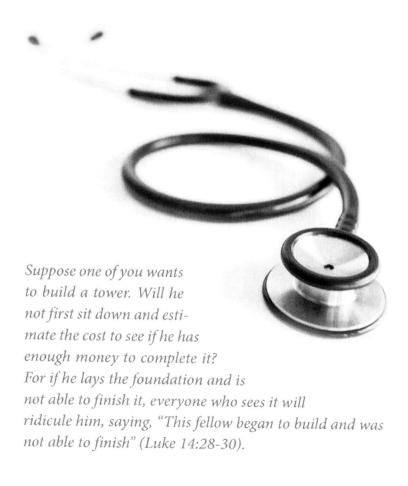

*Suppose one of you wants
to build a tower. Will he
not first sit down and esti-
mate the cost to see if he has
enough money to complete it?
For if he lays the foundation and is
not able to finish it, everyone who sees it will
ridicule him, saying, "This fellow began to build and was
not able to finish" (Luke 14:28-30).*

Chapter 1

Counting the Cost

I N ANY DECISION YOU MAKE, A COST VERSUS BENEFIT analysis occurs. Sometimes it happens in a split second, and you choose that extra helping of ice cream over the amount your thighs will increase. Sometimes you immediately regret these decisions. Other times it takes prayerful deliberation, and a decision might not be made for days, months, even years. It took my wife some two years to agree to even pray about the possibility of dating me. That turned out to be a good thing because I had a lot of areas to grow in before I was ready to date. Good call, God.

Often I hear high school and college students telling me their reasons for wanting to apply to medical school.

To be honest, sometimes it's as if they are deciding what hobby they want to pick up:

"Oh I think I will try out medical school and see if I like it."

"I haven't thought about it too much, but being a doctor seems like a pretty sweet job."

"I like the fact that I get to help people."

"I think medicine is the way to go. I don't really like engineering, law, or business." (This was actually my answer in high school.)

It seems like people spend more time researching what cell phone to get than considering what becoming a doctor actually entails, and what it demands. We can learn a thing or two from Jesus:

> *Large crowds were traveling with Jesus, and turning to them he said: "If anyone comes to me and does not hate his father and mother, his wife and children, his brothers and sisters—yes, even his own life—he cannot be my disciple. And anyone who does not carry his cross and follow me cannot be my disciple. Suppose one of you wants to build a tower. Will he not first sit down and estimate the cost to see if he has enough money to complete it? For if he lays the foundation and is not able to finish it, everyone who sees it will ridicule him, saying, 'This fellow began to build and was not able to finish.'*
>
> *Or suppose a king is about to go to war against another king. Will he not first sit down and consider*

*whether he is able with ten thousand men to oppose
the one coming against him with twenty thousand?
If he is not able, he will send a delegation while the
other is still a long way off and will ask for terms of
peace. In the same way, any of you who does not
give up everything he has cannot be my disciple"
(Luke 14:25-33).*

At this point of His ministry, Jesus was enjoying much
public approval. Large crowds were flocking after Him,
amazed by His teachings, and even more delighted by His
miracles. (What's better than free food during a lecture?
Free food provided miraculously!)

But Jesus knew that many in the crowd did not understand what discipleship involved, so He told them in no
uncertain terms what following Him really meant. In this
passage Jesus makes one of those, "Oh I wish you didn't
say that, Jesus" statements to convey just how all-encompassing following Him is: "If anyone comes to me and
does not hate his father and mother, his wife and children,
his brothers and sisters—yes, even his own life—he cannot be my disciple."

Obviously Jesus doesn't call us to hate our family and
ourselves in the way we may hate child molestation, slav-
ery, and black licorice. Jesus elsewhere calls us to love our
enemies, and the over-arching message of Scripture is that
we love God by loving others. Jesus here is redefining our
familial loyalties and making the point that a true disciple
must consider Jesus more valuable than anything else, including those things (or people) that are the most

precious.⁴ Until we have counted that cost and are willing to potentially give all of that up, Jesus says don't even bother being my disciple. Like someone estimating the cost of a building project, or a king taking stock of his army before a war, let's figure out if we can afford the whole thing before starting the project.

Jesus calls us to consider deeply the costs of discipleship. It's going to demand one's total devotion and willingness to sacrifice everything for the sake of Christ, just as Christ gave His life and endured the cross for the sake of God's kingdom plan. And implied in this passage is that Jesus is worth it, that the value of having Jesus and His kingdom far outweighs the things precious to us and our own ambitions and dreams.

We were all created to live forever with God in perfect intimacy and fellowship. But all of us, since Adam and Eve, have subsequently sinned and rebelled against God. Instead of living in perfect fellowship with our Creator, we are now separated from Him and destined for death. This is not just a physical death, but a spiritual death of eternal separation in hell.

The Bible tells us there is no way to restore our relationship with God except through Jesus Christ, who lived a perfect life and died on the cross as payment for our sins. And through confessing our sins and trusting in Jesus as our Lord and Savior, we are made right before God and we can have a restored relationship with Him. That's the great prize. But what's the cost?

Following Jesus might mean you become alienated from your non-believing family. It might mean you do not get ahead in life because you refuse to cheat. It might mean suffering physically for the sake of the Gospel, even to the point of death. Or getting made fun of at school for reading your Bible and praying. Or being denied an academic promotion because you believe in intelligent design. Discipleship with Christ may demand all those things, but to have Christ is to have God, meeting the deepest need of our souls. That is worth more than anything this world can offer.

"Wait a second," you protest. I thought we were talking about applying to medical school. How did you slip the Gospel in here! (Tricky tricky.) Well, it's relevant because this is the first decision that you need to make in order to make any sense of the rest of your life. Your decision about Christ and what you make Him to be will shape every other decision.

> Discipleship demands one's total devotion and willingness to sacrifice everything for the sake of Christ.

If you are not a Christian, figure this out before you try to figure out anything else. How you live this life depends on what you believe about the next. If this life is all there is, then it might not be a bad idea to work hard for a time to amass great wealth so you can enjoy the rest of your life. The apostle Paul agrees that if Jesus was not raised from the dead, then Christianity is useless. He says in 1 Corinthians 15:32, "If the dead are not raised, 'Let us eat and drink, for tomorrow we die.'" But if Jesus did rise from the dead, proving His claim to be the Son of God, then we better make the right decision about Him.

True Saving Faith

If you are a Christian, you need to make sure you really are a disciple of Jesus. By that I mean not just an "Oh, I believe in Jesus and I like going to church" disciple, but a "Jesus is my Lord and number one priority in my life; I am willing to give up everything for Him" disciple. A multitude of people followed Jesus when He was popular. After the crucifixion, there were little more than a hundred believers left (Acts 1:15).

Just because we prayed a prayer once upon a time accepting Christ into our hearts doesn't necessarily mean we have a saving relationship with Him. Saving faith is trusting the right object for the right reason. It is trusting Jesus, the Son of God (the right object) for the forgiveness of my sins (the right reason) in order to be made right with God. Sounds simple, but people put their trust in many things, don't they? We trust in our possessions, abilities, or our good works (some their good looks). But none of these things can do anything about the sin that separates us from God. We need to trust Jesus, the perfect sacrifice, who died on the cross for those sins we have committed and will commit.

Unfortunately, people also trust in Jesus for all sorts of other reasons. Some come to Jesus because they have a lot of problems, maybe health issues or financial troubles, and they need someone to fix them. Some come because they are lonely, or they enjoy church. Of course our God is able to answer prayers in our times of need and, as believers, we belong to a church body, but these are just the benefits of knowing God through Jesus. The main reason we come to Jesus has to be for the forgiveness of our sins. Otherwise, when our prayers don't get answered the "right" way, or people at church hurt us (and they probably will), or we don't "feel" close to God anymore, we will be hugely tempted to turn our backs on God.

This is a danger even for those of us who have considered ourselves Christians for a long time. Growing up, I never had a problem with the idea that God existed, but I rarely felt a need for Him. I got by life by myself pretty okay (so I thought, anyway). I trusted in my abilities and took a lot of pride in my grades, tennis, and violin; these were the things I was good at. If you met me in high school before I became a Christian, you probably wouldn't have liked me. I was really cocky and critical, looking down on everyone. After I accepted Christ, that attitude did slowly change (praise the Lord), so now I'm just a little less of a jerk.

But this self-sufficiency carried over to my faith. I will talk more about the dangers of trusting in our own abilities and how medicine sets us up to fall big time in a later chapter. Cognitively, I received the gospel, but I didn't really know what it meant to come to Jesus for the forgiveness for my sins. I came to Jesus more for the love I experienced at church and the fulfillment I got from the opportunities to serve. I would eventually get heavily involved in ministry, but instead of relating to God through relationship with Jesus, I tried to relate to God by doing things for Him.

It wasn't really until I was in medical school that I started to see I didn't have much of a relationship with Jesus. When I moved away for medical school, all of a sudden I no longer had my church family, opportunities to serve, the status of being a church leader, or feelings of being needed. Combined with the pressures of school, my spiritual life really tanked. Somehow I had missed the fact that doing the things of God doesn't mean having a real relationship with God. I had not come to Jesus for the right reasons.

> Your decision about Christ and what you make Him to be will shape every other decision.

I think the main issue that prevented me from embracing Jesus as Lord was I really believed I was essentially good, meaning (I wouldn't admit this out loud) when God looked at me without the blood of Christ, I thought He would be pleased. And this was still my belief many years after I prayed to accept Christ. In my head I knew we were all sinners, but in my heart I believed I was better than most, and that was good enough for God.

Deep down we may think, *I'm not so bad. I am definitely better than those "real" sinners like rapists, murderers, and child molesters, and certainly I am not worse than the people around me. They do the same things I do.* We are so busy comparing ourselves with ourselves we forget the ultimate standard: God is perfect, and even one sin is enough to condemn us to hell.

But none of us has committed merely one sin, have we? I've only started to get my mind around my sinfulness in the last several years. A large part was through my relationship with Priscilla. You want to discover ugly things about yourself? Get married. It isn't that Priscilla has super perfect standards that are impossible to live up to. It's easy in a big group to fool people (and yourself) into thinking that you are patient, loving, and considerate. You can just ignore those people who annoy you and put on your happy face.

But when you invite a spouse into your life on that level of intimacy, it's hard to hide your imperfections. It's hard to think you are considerate and loving when you see firsthand how your actions hurt someone you really love, even if "you didn't mean to." And each fight just highlights over and over again that we live in a sinful, fallen world, and we are both sinners, in need of a savior. This is what Christianity is about; this is the heart of the gospel.

One big tragedy in the way we do evangelism is that we are good at describing the secondary blessings of being united with God. It's easy to talk about the love in the church family, or the fulfillment one can find in God, or how our God answers prayers (all true things). But, we are not so good at talking about our sins in a way that is helpful to open people's eyes to their need for God. Another tragedy is that many people come away thinking they are Christians simply because they prayed the sinner's prayer or they come to church every week and do God stuff.

We need to explain what it means to accept Christ, to believe in Him for the forgiveness of our sins. Our deep need is to be reconciled with our Creator God. When we realize that God has purchased us by the blood of His precious Son, then we will start to see that this life is not about us.

God's will is not that we will have a fun time now as a new creation. Jesus calls us instead to deny ourselves, take up our cross, and follow. This means completely devoting to Christ, giving up the way we used to live, and seeking first God's eternal kingdom.

Back to Medicine

Why am I making such a big deal of this? Because medicine is going to make a very similar demand on your life as well. When you choose the medical path, you are also embarking on an all-encompassing journey that will demand of you one hundred percent if you let it, sometimes more. There will be times when you will be asked to choose your studies and duties over your friends, over your family, over your spouse, over your own self-care and recreation, and even over your God.

This is going to be true for any career that you choose to pursue, to varying degrees. The reality is that any job can become an idol, if it is pursued for our own glory and gain. Satan dangles the false promises of the American Dream, and many will forsake much in a vain attempt to obtain it. We will unpack this more in the next chapter.

The sad truth is many in those moments will choose the demands of medicine (or any other career) if they have not made up in their minds what they will not give up. You don't have to look very far to find strained relationships, broken marriages, neglected kids, and spiritual emptiness. Looking back, I would say medical school was one of the darkest times of my life, and I don't know how I would have survived residency had it not been for the support of my wife (then girlfriend) and church family.

You can't just *try out* medicine without counting the cost. At the very minimum it will be a waste of time, energy, and money, but usually more things are at stake. So do your homework. Don't go into medicine because your parents want you to, or you just want to check it out. Talk to as many people as you can at different stages of training. Find out what they wished they had known and what they had to give up. And don't even consider it until you have made your decision about Christ. Figure out if Jesus really is Lord of your life.

We all know medical education is costly, and it takes a long time to get through all the training. According to the American Medical Association, the average medical school debt in 2011 was $162,000 to $205,674.[5] That could be a nice down-payment for a house. Residency training is usually anywhere from three to seven years after medical school. And the training may get even longer because residents, particularly those in surgical fields, are not getting as much experience as a result of all the work-hour restrictions.

What about the less tangible costs? The weekends and summers spent in prep classes, research internships, and hospital volunteering. Unfortunately, life goes on without you, and there were plenty of important events like marriages and family vacations that I missed because I had to study or couldn't get the days off. Now clearly, in the big picture, your career is more important than birthday parties, church retreats, and snowboarding trips. Yet, at the end of your life, what will be more important to you won't be your degree and how much money you have made. It'll be your relationships, those with God and with God's people, and for sure medical training will have emotional and spiritual implications that affect these as well. Much more on this as we go along.

*   *   *

We are all created by God to participate in His kingdom work. As believers, we have been gifted in different ways, and with the power of the Holy Spirit, we are to continue Jesus' ministry of making God known and making disciples of Christ. All of us will live forever, the only question is where. How we live this life will have significant impact on where we will spend eternity, and not just us, but those God has put in our spheres of influence. But, Satan is doing his job well, and many people, including professing Christians, are chasing the empty promises of this world. For some, medicine has become a spiritual death-trap where good intentions turn into building our own castles in the sand.

If you are not a Christian, my prayer is that you would consider the person of Jesus and come to terms with the

Bible's claims about Him. If you are a Christian, please take some time of self-reflection and pray with an open heart about how God would use you with the gifts He has given you. Not all are called to medicine (or engineering or law). If you think it has to be medicine or nothing, then maybe Jesus isn't calling the shots in your life.

If you are a Christian and you are pretty sure God is calling you into medicine, my prayer is that you would hold on to your love for Jesus above all other loves. If He is not number one in your life, then, instead of experiencing the joy that comes with participating in God's kingdom work, you will be sucked into the rat-race, chasing after the American Dream like the rest of the world. And what a waste that will be, to have filled out all those Scantron bubbles for nothing of ultimate significance.

Reflection Questions

1. Have you considered how long medical training is? Take a moment to research the cost of medical education, the amount of time it takes to become different types of doctors, and how much residents make.

2. What have you had to give up so far in your pursuit of medicine? Has it interfered with your relationships, your health, or your faith?

3. What does it mean to be a disciple of Jesus? What demands does Jesus have on those who want to follow Him?

Chapter 2

I Want Money
and Fame!

EVERYONE IS IN MEDICINE FOR THE MONEY, I DON'T care what they say. It may not be the primary motivation and certainly people won't say it that way, but everyone takes into consideration the income and lifestyle promises that is in medicine (especially with the economy the way it is). Oh, and don't forget about the prestige. It's the age-old quest for fame and fortune.

Why do so many forsake so much trying to obtain these things? Well, because we have a deep need for security and significance. Before sin entered into the world, we enjoyed both as God's creation and His image bearers. In the garden there was perfect relationship between God, man, and nature. Nature offered the fruits of the land to eat and man had dominion over all the animals. Adam and Eve had perfect intimacy, and were naked together without shame. Adam walked and talked with God without fear of His wrath and was appointed a caretaker of His creation.

The happy story doesn't last for long, though. Because of their rebellion, Adam and Eve were banished from the garden. The earth no longer bore its fruit so easily and man would have to toil and sweat for food. People began to kill one another, beginning with Cain and Abel. Of course mankind's relationship with God was broken, and God's judgment and wrath was in store for every person.

Without God, people quickly turned to other things for security and significance. Do you remember the story of the tower of Babel? After the flood, God told Noah and his family to go and fill the earth. Several pages later, we find the early people settling down instead. In Genesis 11:4 the people said, "Come, let us build ourselves a city, with a tower that reaches to the heavens, so that we may *make a name for ourselves and not be scattered over the face of the whole earth*" (emphasis added). They wanted fame and security, desiring to be like God and not to be lost in the world.[6] Apart from God, we have all been searching for these same things in what our hands can accomplish, from the tower of Babel to our 401(k)s.

Insecurity as a result of our broken relationship with God is obvious. As a family physician, anxiety is one of the most common patient complaints I get. Some patients are so anxious you can feel the tension walking into the room. Think about the amount of money we spend on insurance policies. There are warranties on the products we buy, car insurance, health insurance, home insurance, earthquake insurance, life insurance, and disability insurance.

And what's left over goes to building up our savings for retirement. The mindset of the world is this: Make a lot of money and protect what you worked so hard to earn. Employ multiple strategies to prevent the government from taking too much tax away so that, at the end, you can enjoy what your hands have accomplished and not worry about being in need.

Isn't that what everyone is working for, both Christians and non-Christians? Work hard, buy a house, pay off the mortgage, put children through college, and save up and invest wisely so you can have a nice retirement to enjoy the rest of your years playing tennis, taking walks, and spoiling your grandchildren. That sounds like a pretty good life, yeah? That's the American Dream! Is this a worthwhile goal to pursue? Let's see if Jesus has anything relevant to say about it:

Someone in the crowd said to him, "Teacher, tell my brother to divide the inheritance with me."

Jesus replied, "Man, who appointed me a judge or an arbiter between you?"

Then he said to them, "Watch out! Be on your guard against all kinds of greed; a man's life does not consist in the abundance of his possessions."

And he told them this parable: "The ground of a certain rich man produced a good crop. He thought to himself, 'What shall I do? I have no place to store my crops.'

"Then he said, 'This is what I'll do. I will tear down my barns and build bigger ones, and there I will store all my grain and my goods. And I'll say to myself, "You have plenty of good things laid up for many years. Take life easy; eat, drink and be merry."'

"But God said to him, 'You fool! This very night your life will be demanded from you. Then who will get what you have prepared for yourself?'

"This is how it will be with anyone who stores up things for himself but is not rich toward God" (Luke 12:13-21).

Here Jesus was teaching in a crowd and someone brought up an inheritance dispute he was having with his brother. Jesus wasn't interested in fixing the problem, but did take this opportunity to teach on the underlying issue—the brother's greed in seeking earthly possessions. Jesus proceeded to tell this parable of a rich man who had a great harvest that year. Notice that this man was already rich and Jesus didn't make any moral judgments. The guy's just a rich person who had a good harvest; nothing wrong with that.

But now this rich guy had a dilemma. He didn't have enough room for all this new stuff. It was a real problem. It was a nice problem to have! Still nothing wrong here. So he thought a bit and came up with the solution—he decided to tear down his old barns and build bigger ones so that he could have room for everything. Sounds logical, right? More stuff needs more space. Still, we find no hints of judgment or im-

> Medicine can become a spiritual death-trap where good intentions turn into building castles in the sand.

morality, although we do get a sense of his selfishness. Look at the number of personal pronouns: "my" crops, "my" barns, "I" will store, "my" grain, and "my" goods.

The main issue was his reasoning for building bigger barns: "And I'll say to myself, 'You have plenty of good things laid up for many years. Take life easy; eat, drink and be merry.'" He was going to find comfort and security in his increasing wealth so he could take it easy and enjoy the rest of his life. Immediately after that decision, God showed up and told the fellow that he would not get to enjoy what he had planned to hoard for himself. That very night God would take his life. What's the moral of the story? Are we going to be rich toward ourselves, holding on to our possessions for our own comfort and security, or are we going to be rich toward God?[7]

Now I don't know about you, but, "And I'll say to myself, 'You have plenty of good things laid up for many years.

Take life easy, eat, drink and be merry'" sounds awfully a lot to me like the American Dream that I just described. And remember, in this passage Jesus is warning against greed. Before you let yourself off the hook because you don't cheat and screw others over to get rich, realize that in this parable Jesus doesn't depict someone like that. Here's a man who happens to be rich, who happens to have gotten a good return on his crops this year, and he wants to plan so that he can enjoy what his hands have produced. That's a very different picture of greed than what we are used to.

Another problem we run into is that we don't typically see greed as that bad, at least not as bad as murdering or sexually assaulting people. But Scripture is clear that greed is not a small thing. In fact, it is actually idolatry. Ephesians 5:5 says, "For of this you can be sure: No immoral, impure, or greedy person—such a man is an idolater—has any inheritance in the kingdom of Christ and of God." The Bible puts greed on the same level as sexual immorality and impurity. Do you see greed in that way?

The relevant question for us is this: Are you rich toward yourself or are you rich toward God? Are you going to be more preoccupied building your own kingdom here on earth or building God's heavenly kingdom? In Christ there is the promise of the eternal. Christ will come again and those who are found in Him will be with Him forever. We don't think about eternity nearly enough, or we think sub-par thoughts of an eternity consisting of clouds, baby angels, and harps.

Do we realize the time we have on this earth is just the very beginnings of our existence? After this life is over, those found in Christ will be united with their Creator God as His children, enjoying His presence, perfect peace, perfect love, no sickness, no tears, and no more sin. It is the fulfillment of why we were created. Yet the majority of people on this earth, both Christians and non-Christians alike, spend the majority of their time, energy, and resources building up their little temporary earthly kingdom without any regard for eternity or the things that have eternal consequences. Let's not forget that Jesus is coming back.

Are We Ready?

I once cared for a pregnant patient who had irregular periods, so I wasn't quite sure when her baby was coming. Her estimated due date came and went, and the weeks continued to go by. As each week passed I got more and more anxious because I had no idea when she was going to deliver.

I had to completely change my schedule around because I was anticipating this delivery. I passed up on different trips because I couldn't leave town. When I went to sleep I had my little bag ready with my scrubs and toiletries in case I needed to leave in the middle of the night. I made sure I always had my pager because, of course, it would be after hours, and probably while I was doing something fun.

Sure enough, I got a page one night while I was out eating with my family so I had to scarf down my food and rush to the hospital. I got there and examined her, relieved to find her looking pretty comfortable, but definitely in labor. To speed things up a tad, I broke her amniotic sac and after, took a quick nap. An hour later, she was further along but still not quite ready to push.

Judging from her progress, I figured we probably had another hour or so before we could encourage her to start pushing. I thought about going downstairs to take another nap, but then decided to hang out on the floor. On a whim I went into her room soon after that discussion just to check some stuff and she was looking like she was in a lot of pain, wanting to push. I told her she wasn't ready yet, but then she had that look like something was coming. So I decided to look, and sure enough there was the baby's head about to come out.

I had about ten seconds to catch this baby. Thankfully it was just enough time to throw on some gloves. The delivery went well and everything was great, but it just struck me how sudden the whole process could be. There are stories of doctors who don't make it in time and the mom delivers the baby on the bed. Or women who thought they had to defecate but out comes a baby instead in the bathroom. It's so unpredictable; we just have to be ready.

Doesn't the Bible describe the second coming of Christ kind of like that? Paul writes in 1 Thessalonians 5:1-3, "Now, brothers, about times and dates we do not need to write to you, for you know very well that the day of the Lord will come like a thief in the night. While people are saying, 'Peace and safety,' destruction will come on them suddenly, as labor pains on a pregnant woman, and they will not escape." Christ is coming back, and I hope we won't be caught unawares.

Are you ready for Christ's return? Do you have your "spiritual" bags packed? Have you been made right with God and other people? Do you live your life around the fact that Jesus will come back? That doesn't mean we just sit around and neglect our day-to-day responsibilities. Paul has much to say to people who think that way, especially in his letters to the Thessalonians. But we have to understand that we live for eternity and so we make our everyday choices accordingly.

I once met a fellow believer involved in local politics who slept with a travel bag near his bed. He did that to remind himself that he's just passing through in this life so not to get too settled in this world. We need more people like him, not just Christians in politics, but Christians who are eternally minded.

Treasures in Heaven

Yes, there are important things in this world. Paying your mortgage is important. Figuring out your 401(k) is important. Providing for your family is important. The Bible does teach stewardship of our resources and that we will be held accountable for what we have been given.

But what is most important is that we are right in our relationship with God. Because even if, God forbid, we are no longer able to make the mortgage payments, or our retirement fund crashes with the stock market, or if we are not able to support our future family, in the end, in Christ, we will have eternal treasures in God in heaven.

Even if all these earthly disasters were to happen, we have the promise from God not just of a heavenly inheritance to come, but also of God's earthly provision of the basic needs of His children now, just as He clothes the grass of the fields and feeds the birds of the air. That's the passage right after this parable (and more on this in Chapter 10).

Now, I do want to say that there's nothing wrong with having wealth. First Timothy 6:10 tells us money is not the root of all evil, but the love of money is the issue. God blesses, at times, with riches. Remember, God brought the Israelites into Canaan, the land flowing with milk and honey, where they could settle down and prosper. Under the reign of King David and King Solomon, Israel was a powerful nation with immense riches and wealth. Ministry can get expensive and we need money in order to carry it out. Certain people can only be reached by people who have resources and influence themselves.

> We don't think about eternity nearly enough, or we think sub-par thoughts of an eternity consisting of clouds, baby angels, and harps.

But we have to realize that Scripture has some scary things to say against rich people. All the passages I can think of that address the rich are either warnings against loving their wealth, or a straight out rebuke. Why? Because with money comes the temptation to use that money not for God, but for ourselves, to make our lives more comfortable and secure.

As I have mentioned, it is not uncommon to come out of medical school with over a hundred thousand dollars in debt. Throw in three years (at the minimum) of making a resident's salary and figure in wanting to start a family. Add perhaps a new mortgage of another two hundred thousand dollars to all of this, and that initial fire to forsake it all for the kingdom by going into missions, or serve the homeless, or whatever else you had in mind with medicine, gets doused just a bit.

Maybe more than just a bit. It is not all that surprising why certain specialties have trouble filling their training spots, particularly primary care fields. I'm no economic expert, but it seems like choice of specialty is influenced pretty significantly by the amount of money that can be made. And the salary differential between different specialties can be quite substantial.

It all goes back to the question of what or who is number one in your life. Is Jesus calling the shots, or do you defer to your desires for security and fame? Follow your heart and pursue the American Dream, and you might have a pretty sweet life with a nice house, 2.3 kids, and a cushy savings account. You might attend church every Sunday and even serve on a regular basis. But take care that you don't mistake simply adding Jesus to the end of your work week with a life of discipleship. Do not be deceived into thinking just because you attach Jesus' name to the end of your priority list, you are actually following His.

A book that exposes the grip the American Dream has on Christians is David Platt's wonderfully relevant *Radical: Taking Back Your Faith From the American Dream.* He writes that many have created for themselves a Jesus they would like to follow, rather than the Jesus portrayed by the Bible. He challenges our pursuit of comfort and security and reminds us the radical commitment Christ calls us to is actually "normal" Christianity.[8]

On the other hand, you might go through the whole process and realize that fulfillment doesn't come with an MD and a mortgage. As I've said, becoming a doctor isn't all sunshine and marshmallows, and even after your training is done, all your problems don't go away. *Newsweek* put out an article in 2008 titled "Doctors Who Kill Themselves" where they report that some three hundred to four hundred doctors commit suicide yearly—more than any other profession.[9] I personally knew of one.

Count the cost. Jesus says in Matthew 16:24-26, "If anyone would come after me, he must deny himself and take up his cross and follow me. For whoever wants to save his life will lose it, but whoever loses his life for me will find it. What good will it be for a man if he gains the whole world, yet forfeits his soul? Or what can a man give in exchange for his soul?" Watch out that you don't trade your soul for a dream.

Reflection Questions

1. Have you felt the need for significance and security in your life? How have you tried to meet those needs?

2. What have people been willing to give up in order to obtain the American Dream? What are you willing to give up?

3. How can realizing our identity as God's children free us from the endless rat-race that dominates our society?

Chapter 3

I Want to
Help People!

THE TRICKIEST PART ABOUT WRITING A PERSONAL statement and doing a medical school interview is to figure out a way to say you want to help people without sounding naïvely cliché and having your evaluators roll their eyes. And then you have to figure out how to say it again in a different way when you apply for residency.

I think everyone who goes into medicine does want to help people, some more than others. I've had the pleasure of meeting some of the most compassionate people I know through medical school and residency. Like many others, I had a desire to truly care for those who are suffering. Carrying that out, though, was something else altogether.

Not to sound all holy, but one of my inspirations for the kind of doctor I wanted to be was Jesus and how He healed. Jesus in His ministry didn't care only about spiritual healing, but He showed a concern for total restoration, which included also the physical and emotional. One account in particular that brings me back to the true meaning of health is Jesus' interaction with the leper in Mark 1. I actually wrote about this in my personal statement when applying to medical school:

A man with leprosy came to him and begged him on his knees, "If you are willing, you can make me clean."

Filled with compassion, Jesus reached out his hand and touched the man. "I am willing," he said. "Be clean!" Immediately the leprosy left him and he was cured.

Jesus sent him away at once with a strong warning: "See that you don't tell this to anyone. But go, show yourself to the priest and offer the sacrifices that Moses commanded for your cleansing, as a testimony to them" (Mark 1:40-44).

Biblical authors used the term "leprosy" to describe a variety of chronic skin conditions, not necessarily referring to Hansen's disease as we know it today.[10] Leviticus 13:1-46 details how people with such diseases were to be dealt with. According to the Mosaic Law, anyone with a skin disease that did not resolve was considered unclean. Like the laws that govern cooties, any contact with a leper made you unclean as well. Consequently, those with skin diseases were forced to live away from the city to avoid contaminating other people. Worse yet, they had to dress in a way that made it clear they were unclean. And if you still didn't get the warning, they had to walk around yelling, "Unclean! Unclean!"

Leviticus 13:46 poignantly sums up this man's predicament: "As long as he has the infection he remains unclean. He must live alone; he must live outside the camp." You can imagine not just the physical suffering of having the illness, but also the emotional pains from being isolated and stigmatized.

And the culture didn't have any of this "watch out for yourself" attitude. To the first century Jew, the community, and particularly the religious community, was a big deal. Obviously, this kind of lifestyle precluded the leper from involvement at the temple, and no temple meant no God. Here we find a man with physical suffering, emotional pain, and spiritual separation. In one amazing encounter with Jesus, every need was met in one fell swoop as they say.

Jesus could have healed this man in any way imaginable. He could have wiggled His pinky, or even thought about wiggling His pinky, and the leprous man would have been healed. Yet in compassion, Jesus saw the depths of the man's pain and Mark made it a point to include this little detail: Jesus reached out and touched the man. The scandal! Here was a supposedly upright, God-fearing rabbi touching a known, unclean leper? But Jesus remained clean, and immediately the man was cured. You can imagine the power of that touch, drawing the man back into human contact and relationship.

And Jesus didn't stop there. He told the man to go to the temple to do the things prescribed by Moses in order to show he was cured of the disease and clean according to the laws. This allowed the man to be reincorporated into the community and, more importantly, into the religious life. God cares about the physical, emotional, and spiritual and He commands His people to care about the same.

Non-medical Medical Problems

I wanted to be that kind of doctor, to be able to see past the physical and meet the deeper needs of my patients, which was another reason family medicine appealed to me. Looking back, that was a great attitude when I had two hours as a medical student to see a patient. I could talk about all sorts of things. But now in fifteen minute slots I am expected to address patient concerns, manage chronic conditions, keep updated an ever increasing list of health maintenance

> I had a desire to truly care for those who are suffering. Carrying that out, though, was something else altogether.

tasks, perform a physical exam, educate patients on the care plan and medications, and do all of this with active listening and empathy, partnering with patients to motivate them to take charge of their health—sometimes doing all this through a translator phone.

It was estimated in 2003 that a physician would need seven-plus hours per day to complete all the recommended preventative services for a typical patient panel, and another ten-plus hours per day to provide quality long-term care.[11] With ever-improving technology we can do a lot of things quicker and more efficiently, but that just means more things are squeezed into the time that's freed up. No wonder studies have shown physicians have higher rates of burnout compared to non-medical professionals, with the highest burnout among adult primary care providers.[12]

The reality is that the current system encourages reactive and defensive medicine, with physicians scrambling to meet productivity quotas and countless quality indicators. As much as we hate to admit it, fears of malpractice lawsuits and economic concerns do influence the way healthcare is delivered and the freedom a physician has to care for patients.

The other reality is the changing nature of medicine and disease. It didn't take very long after medical school for me to figure out that patients came to the office with problems that were not strictly medical, and I wasn't equipped to handle the real issues that came my way. Sometimes I honestly wonder if what I do even makes much of a difference.

It used to be that people went to their doctors because of something that happened to them—they got an infection, an animal attacked them, or they got injured somehow by their environment. These were mostly things outside of their control, which is probably still the case in non-industrialized nations. Nowadays, the majority of disease that I see every day in my office is, for the most part, a consequence of lifestyle choices, things that patients do to themselves as a result of their behavior.

Think about the top three killers in the United States: cardiovascular disease, cancer, and lower respiratory diseases.[13] We would make a huge dent in these if people simply ate better, stopped smoking, and exercised more. The majority of the disease burden of the twenty-first century in industrialized nations is chronic illness that are either caused by or made worse by poor self-care.

And these chronic conditions impact not just the patient, but they also create a lot of stress and strain in the person's relationships. When people realize they have hurt themselves and the ones they love because of their own personal choices, then they start to experience such things as guilt, regret, shame, and worthlessness.

So when patients come in, they don't come in with just physical complaints (they may think that's all they have). In addition, they have the emotional and spiritual burden of disease that I, a medical doctor, am very poorly trained to address. The mind is a powerful and mysterious thing. Sometimes the physical symptoms are simply the manifestations of emotional and spiritual turmoil that the patient is experiencing. All the known diagnostic tests can come back normal, yet the patient can have very real and debilitating physical pain. And that's why I believe that even though there has been (and continues to be) an explosion of medical advances, I am not doing much good to my patients if all I focus on is the physical.

Yes, I can temporarily treat things by prescribing this medication to control your blood pressure, or that medication for your diabetes, or this other medication to make you not feel so sad. But what I am mostly doing is just treating the symptoms, rather than the root causes of these problems. Sometimes I feel like all I am doing is giving out big sophisticated bandages. Or being a glorified janitor, as Dr. Nick would say, mopping up the mess today, only to have to do it again and again. We operate in a system that provides sickcare, not healthcare.

The solution to the experiences of guilt, shame, and worthlessness isn't found in pill form, but involves words such as forgiveness, redemption, restoration, and grace. Modern medicine cannot provide the answer because these are spiritual needs first and foremost.[14] They certainly don't teach you how to handle this in medical school. That's why more and more, as a general doctor, I wish not only could there be specialists right in my office, but there could be a pastor or church worker as well who can go deeper with patients after I have identified a spiritual need, or simply pray with patients and provide additional support.

Having said that, it could be tempting to think, *I'm a medical doctor so I'll just focus on the medical stuff. I don't have much time anyway so I'll leave the spiritual healing to the pastors and other "professional" Christians.* No, as a physician, you are at such a strategic position to bridge the gap between the physical and the spiritual. Remember, Jesus preached God's kingdom and healed every sickness and disease. He was essentially a pastor *and* a doctor; those callings are intimately connected. I will talk more about providing spiritual care in the next chapter.

Burnout

As Christian physicians, we have many wonderful opportunities to, at the very least, start the conversation. It's been a great joy to be able to pray with some of my patients. But I need to point out, frankly, that by the time we get to residency training and beyond, we might not even care anymore. Medical school demands our time, our mind, and our energy. It also demands our emotional investment, and sometimes we just don't have much left over to give to our patients.

You are training to be a healer, and you are expected to have the answers, to provide the comfort, to pour out each and every time. And to do it again the next day. Unfortunately, medical school doesn't teach you very well how to fill up. In fact, people learn to neglect things that fill them in order to pass a class or get a better grade—things like faith, family, and hobbies, the very things that we tell our patients not to neglect.

Here's a journal entry I wrote halfway through intern year. By the way, if you don't journal, I highly recommend taking up the practice. I changed the details to protect the identities of the patients.

> Wow . . . six months of intern year has passed already. Hardest couple months I have to agree . . .

and more hard ones to go. I've learned a whole lot
... but am I less human? less loving? less compassionate? I can't even take a moment to cry for Mrs.
Smith, without family or friends at her deathbed,
kept alive against her wishes because psych
deemed her incapable to make decisions. Or for
Mr. Kim's family asking for any sort of hope to
hang on to before pulling the plug. How about Mr.
Johnson or Ms. Gonzalez, or those two that coded
and died while I did CPR on them, breaking their
ribs. I don't even know their names. And the next
day I'm expected to do it all over again, to greet
the patients who are alive with compassion and
warmth. How am I going to last three years?

You would think doctors-in-training would come out of
training more compassionate and loving toward their patients, but more often than not, cynicism grows instead. At
the end of a thirty-hour shift or an eighty-hour work week,
I honestly cared much more about getting home so I could
sleep than about my patients' emotional and spiritual health.
I think medical schools and residency programs are recog-
nizing this, with new work hour restrictions and more emphasis on self-care and physician well-being. But it's a culture
that's going to be hard to change since physicians are typically the "pull your boots up by the bootstraps" type. I can't
even imagine the experience of the previous generation of
physicians who didn't have any work hour restrictions.

Before we have grandiose dreams of healing our patients through our love for them, let's make sure we have

a relationship with the source of love. Romans 5:8 says, "But God demonstrates his own love for us in this: while we were still sinners, Christ died for us." The Bible teaches that God's love is on a whole different level from ours. It is the love that prompted Jesus to step down from His heavenly dwelling to incarnate in weakness, to suffer at the hands of man so that He could die on the cross and be raised, rescuing us even while we were happily indulging in sin.

Saving Ourselves

Here we need to take care because, as people who have hearts to do good, we are tempted to mistake doing good for being good. Like I said earlier, in medicine I have met the nicest, most compassionately self-giving people in my life, many of whom are not Christians. One of my classmates, after completing his training, created his own nonprofit organization to personally provide medical care in areas of Haiti devastated by the 2010 earthquake. I am so inspired by the goodness and courage I have seen in my fellow colleagues to battle suffering and injustice.

But what do generally good people say when presented with their need for a savior? "Why? I'm a good person." Essentially, what they are saying is, "My goodness will get me into heaven." But the Bible is clear that even at our best, we are like "filthy rags" to God (Isaiah 64:6). We need to watch out, because if we do not grasp the depths of our sinfulness, then our hearts will be closed to the love of

God and the central message of the gospel that we are saved by grace alone through faith in Jesus Christ.

This is where medical training can be particularly dangerous to our spiritual life. Essentially, medical training is a training to reject God. I was going to say medical training sends people on their way to hell, but I didn't think readers would take that very well. But that is kind of what it does. To be fair, every human endeavor and secular training can lead people away from God. (This can happen even in seminary training!) But I think medicine specifically poses great dangers. Let me explain.

> God cares about the physical, emotional, and spiritual and He commands His people to care about the same.

The subject matter and method of the training condition pre-med students to think apart from God. With most budding physicians scientifically inclined in the first place, by the time they get through college, their worldview has been so ingrained by the scientific method that it is through that lens they relate with God. Even if there is no outright rejection of God, there is always a lingering doubt about an all-powerful being who is supernatural. Some Christians may profess faith in God, but when it comes to the things outside of what science can measure, our inner heart is asking, "Where's the proof?"

I have to admit that even though intellectually I believe God can do anything, whenever I hear about a miraculous healing, the very first thought that crosses my mind is, "It was probably misdiagnosed." It is hard for me to pray in faith for healing because I know that's just not how it works according to the laws of nature. It's much easier for me to depend on the medicines we have than on God, who is the Creator of life. I forget that God actually created those laws I am so counting on.

This is a sad reality because the study of science should actually point us to the beauty, majesty, and wisdom of God. Psalm 19 expresses how nature declares in no uncertain terms God's amazing qualities, and the human body is no exception. Even the individual cell has an intricacy that the best engineer would be envious of, let alone how every cell comes together to make up a human being. Creation screams intelligent design, yet if that is even mentioned in schools, it is done in a way that is derisive and simply pooh-poohed away.

Even though our faith is based on objective, verifiable truth, not everything in life can be so easily measured. If God can be simply explained by our human intellect, then He would not be much of a God. Unfortunately, science has been falsely elevated as the ultimate judge of truth, and as a result, medical education trains a person to live by sight, not by faith. It also trains the person to depend on the self.

I will touch more on this in a later chapter, but medicine is a celebration of individual accomplishment, and to become a doctor is not a small thing. Of course there is support from family and friends but, ultimately, it is self-determination that wins the day. And with every obstacle that is overcome, it is just another reinforcement of "Yes, I can do it!"

It's easy to forget that the night before the MCAT you pled with God to please help you do well on the test.

This is going to be true in any field, that the more you know and the better you get at something, the more you will be tempted to trust in your own power and strength. But there are just so many darn chances in medicine for you to take pride in yourself since it's such a long journey with many obstacles to overcome. Of course the positive reinforcements of your greatness that people give you (and particularly from parents of single children they would like to marry a future doctor) don't help check your burgeoning ego, either.

When we spend our whole life earning accolades based on our own merit, we should not be surprised that the free grace God offers in Jesus means very little. That truth never makes it to the heart because we are so programmed to relate based on what we do. Take a moment and think about this statement: I am acceptable to God if I obey. Is that a "Duh, that's obvious" statement? That certainly sounds right, right? That's the way many of us perceive our parents.

Yes, the Bible says God demonstrates His love for us through Jesus dying on the cross when we were trying to obey but we just needed a little more help. No! Jesus died for us while we were still sinners! While we lived in sin, He loved us and justified us through His Son, Jesus Christ. Every Christian should profess that. Yet many still live as if God's love depends on what we do, that the better a Christian we are, the more God loves us.

Is God displeased by sin? Sure. Are there rewards for obedience? Certainly. But does God's love and acceptance of us change because of how we perform? Absolutely not. We are accepted one hundred percent in God's sight because, not only are all our sins put onto Christ, all of Jesus' righteousness is given to us. There's nothing else we can do to make ourselves more or less acceptable to God. It has already been accomplished through faith in Jesus. This is the amazing truth, that we are justified completely by faith in Jesus. This is what Luther rediscovered that set off the whole Protestant Reformation.

I am in the middle of the slow and painful process of de-constructing my reliance on my own strength and learning to depend fully on Jesus' accomplished work on the cross. I am learning what it means to surrender to God's transforming love for me. And I have to admit, it seems like every cell in my body is trying to resist. I am hugely tempted to make myself good, to justify my standing before God because of how I help people, how much I serve at church, and how much I have given up for God (which really is not much at all). Consequently, the cross has become tiny in my life, making very little difference in my everyday experience with God and people.

We have to look clearly at the depths of our sins from which only the gospel of Jesus can rescue us. That's true saving faith. Anything else is just "God as an add-on" to round out our already accomplished life. That view of God has no saving power, because the trust is fully on oneself. I don't want to presume on anyone's eternal destiny, since our God is mighty to save. But those who don't want to be saved might just get what they don't really want.

* * *

God's love is constant, unfailing and steadfast. Ours is conditional and fickle, influenced by how we feel and think. First we need to respond to God's love for us, and turn from our own efforts at saving ourselves. Jesus then commands His followers, those who have experienced God's love, to love one another as Jesus has loved (John 13:34-35). By the power of the Holy Spirit working within us and as we continue to receive love from God, we can hope to love those who are difficult, and we'll come across plenty of difficult people in whatever career we chose. And even when we don't feel like loving, the love of God in us will help us to go above and beyond, and do it again and again.

Reflection Questions

1. What have you experienced that makes you want to help others who are hurting?

2. In what ways have you seen your love fail or the love of others fail you? What does the Bible say about God's love in Romans 5:8?

3. If you are in medical school or beyond, how has your training affected your love for patients? How can you continue to grow in compassion amidst the pressures of training?

Chapter 4

The Right
Perspective

Y PURPOSE IN WRITING THIS BOOK ISN'T TO RAIN on anyone's parade and crush people's dreams of becoming a doctor. Rather, it is to offer a new perspective, one that is Jesus-centric in which to filter all the decisions we make in life. This chapter should really be called "The Christ Perspective."

Wherever you are at in your medical journey, whether you are just thinking about it, sending off your applications, trying to memorize all the cranial nerves, or already in residency, you have to make a decision about

Jesus and whether or not He is Lord of your life. That involves prayerfully considering if medicine is really where God has called you. That might mean giving up your dreams or even what you have already accomplished for the sake of Christ in order to embrace what God has in store for you.

The reality is that your relationship with Jesus is the most important thing in this life (they didn't teach me this in medical school for sure), because it will determine where you spend the next. Consider the life and teachings of the apostle Paul:

Finally, my brothers, rejoice in the Lord! It is no trouble for me to write the same things to you again, and it is a safeguard for you.

Watch out for those dogs, those men who do evil, those mutilators of the flesh. For it is we who are the circumcision, we who worship by the Spirit of God, who glory in Christ Jesus, and who put no confidence in the flesh—though I myself have reasons for such confidence.

If anyone else thinks he has reasons to put confidence in the flesh, I have more: circumcised on the eighth day, of the people of Israel, of the tribe of Benjamin, a Hebrew of Hebrews; in regard to the law, a Pharisee; as for zeal, persecuting the church; as for legalistic righteousness, faultless.

But whatever was to my profit I now consider loss for the sake of Christ. What is more, I consider everything a loss compared to the surpassing greatness of knowing Christ Jesus my Lord, for whose sake I have lost all things. I consider them rubbish, that I may gain Christ and be found in him, not having a righteousness of my own that comes from the law, but that which is through faith in Christ— the righteousness that comes from God and is by faith. I want to know Christ and the power of his resurrection and the fellowship of sharing in his sufferings, becoming like him in his death, and so, somehow, to attain to the resurrection from the dead (Philippians 3:1-11).

Paul is writing to his beloved church at Philippi, a congregation with which he had a very tender relationship. This church was mostly made up of non-Jews, or Gentiles, who did not grow up with the Mosaic Law. Paul wrote to warn them because there were false teachings going around that a person needed more than the blood of Jesus for the Christian life. False teachers taught that a person needed to follow the laws of Moses, and in particular, that men had to be circumcised in order to really belong to God's family.

For many of us living in the twenty-first century, that is a strange concept. I perform circumcisions in our procedure clinic on occasion, and most are done not for religious reasons. But for the Jews living in the time of Jesus, circumcision was a big deal. It was given by God to His people in Genesis 17 to be a physical sign that separated Israel from the surrounding nations. For the Jews, circumcision became something they placed their hope in, something they thought signified they belonged to God and were His people.

Paul had harsh words reserved for these false teachers, calling them all sorts of names. He argued no, the believers in Jesus Christ, those circumcised in the heart, were the ones who could be confident when standing before God at the final judgment. Paul understood there was nothing apart from faith in Jesus Christ that could make him right before God. But if there was anything on his own that he could have done to earn righteousness before God, then Paul said, "Been there; done that."

To prove it, Paul listed his very impressive résumé. He was circumcised on the eighth day as prescribed by the Old Testament Law. He belonged to God's people, the nation of Israel. On top of that, he was from the tribe of Benjamin, the tribe that gave the nation its first king and the only one that stuck with Judah when the kingdom split. In respect to obedience to God's Law, he was a Pharisee, a group dedicated to preserving and carrying out God's commands. They were so into God they even came up with more rules to obey to keep from breaking the original ones.

> The reality is that your relationship with Jesus is the most important thing in this life . . . because it will determine where you spend the next.

Paul was so zealous in his Judaism that it led him to persecute and put to death those he thought were the enemies of God: the Christians. Paul claimed that in every way that was humanly possible to live in a manner pleasing to God, he was faultless. But looking back at his own résumé, Paul concluded that all his accomplishments were a loss compared to knowing Jesus Christ. He understood that at the judgment seat of God, nothing else was going to matter except for faith in Jesus Christ for the forgiveness of sins.

We will not be able to stand before God on our own accomplishments and efforts. Paul's main point is very simple: Only faith in Jesus Christ could make his relationship right with God. Not circumcision. Not his Jewish background. Not his outstanding training and study. And not doing his best to follow all the rules. None of those things dealt with the sin that separates all of us from God.

For that very reason, Paul considered not just his religious background a loss, but that *everything* had no worth next to knowing Jesus. Nothing else in his life compared to knowing Christ, who was the key to eternal life. Everything else was "rubbish," all worthless.[15]

What does it mean to know Jesus Christ? Part of it is believing that Jesus is the Son of God who died on the cross as punishment for our sins, and was resurrected, having victory over death so that those who believe in Him can have eternal life as well. But when Paul said he wanted to "know Christ and the power of his resurrection and the fellowship of sharing in his sufferings, becoming like him in his death," he included sharing in His sufferings in the definition of knowing Jesus. For the apostle, that meant putting to death his own self and all that he had accomplished in order to live in obedience to God's will for him.

After Paul converted to Christianity on the road to Damascus, God said in Acts 9:16, "I will show him how much he must suffer for my name." How's that for an encouragement to start off your new Christian walk? God chose Paul to be His messenger to the Gentiles, and Paul suffered incredible trials in order to carry that out. If you want to refresh your memory, read 2 Corinthians 11 (there's another impressive résumé). It lists all the hardships Paul endured for the sake of Christ and His gospel.

Paul gave up all that he had accomplished, which, from the Jewish perspective, looked like a pretty amazing life. He gave it all up to embrace the sufferings of Christ because he saw the truth that Jesus was Lord of his life. So, to know Jesus Christ is not only to know about Him, who the Bible says He is, the mere facts about Jesus. It's not even just about believing so you can get a ticket into heaven. But it is making Jesus your number one priority. It is a call to deny yourself in order to submit to God's will for your life, which often involves suffering. Remember, there is a cost to following Jesus.

And so we are back to where we started. Have you counted the cost? Have you come to realize that nothing in this life amounts to anything without having a relationship with Jesus Christ? Until you make that decision, anything you do will ultimately be meaningless regardless of what you accomplish.

Those who have made Jesus their Lord and number one priority are given the privilege of participating in

God's redemptive work here on earth before He returns. Only with Jesus in His rightful place in our hearts can we start asking how we can be used for God's glory. I want to emphasize again that anything we set our hearts to will have costs as well, asking of us our energy, time, and relationships. But this is especially true in the field of medicine. With Christ properly seated in the throne of our hearts, we can pursue whatever vocation God has gifted us for without that becoming an idol in our lives.

Have you prayerfully considered how God has gifted you? Medicine is a great field, but you don't need to go into medicine to help people have better health. There is a huge body of literature that shows a very significant association of societal influences on an individual's health, such as social status and educational level. If you really care about people being physically well, you should actually go into policy making, education, economic planning, poverty reduction, or housing development because these so-called "social determinants of health" impact health much more than whether or not a patient sees a doctor.[16]

By the way, you also don't have to be a doctor to work in the medical field. I try to go on yearly outreaches to Mexico, and usually go with a team of dentists. I have to say, if you are interested in missions, there is a tremendous need for Christian dentists. Most people who came to see us doctors were simply waiting in line to see the dentists. With dentistry, you are able to address an immediate need. And you get dedicated time with the patient where you can talk and they have to listen.

We need Christian teachers, lawyers, engineers, politicians, and artists. We need Christian everythings because God's kingdom is not limited to just one area of society, but is the all-encompassing transformation of every fabric of society. Imagine the kind of kingdom advancement that could be made if the abilities and intellect that accomplished air and space travel, figured out physics, painted the *Mona Lisa*, and erected the Great Wall of China were applied to the work of God and the preaching of the gospel.

But We Do Need Christian Physicians . . .

When I met her she was in DKA, high on cocaine, and angry. She was angry at herself for allowing a small foot wound to develop into a raging osteomyelitis.[17] She was angry with us for telling her she needed an amputation. She was in denial, adamantly refusing the treatment that could save her life. Three weeks later, she was missing a foot but had a smile on her face. On my last day she told me that while the doctors had healed her body, I helped to heal her soul. Knowing her church background, I had offered to pray with her, and that led her to reconnect with God. God reminded her of her worth as a person, motivating her to care for her body. She reminded me that health extends beyond just physical healing.

That was the introduction from my personal statement when I applied to residency. This was a patient encounter that solidified for me the tremendous opportunity for spiritual impact I could have as a physician.

As much as we need Christians in every field, there are some very strategic reasons to be in medicine for the purposes of expanding God's kingdom. A big one is that being a doctor automatically, for some reason, makes you an authority in any subject. Watermelons grow better in the cold and surrounded by strawberries? You are a doctor; what you say must be true! People will listen to you, not so much because of what you say, but because you have a medical degree. I think people assume that since we did all that studying, we must have studied everything.

All kidding aside, as a physician, you do have tremendous influence. People will look to you not just for the answer to their every bodily complaint (in and out of the office), but they will look to you as a role model and for leadership. Physicians have a powerful voice in lobbying because people will listen. Think of the opportunities you can have to impact your community, and even the nation, if you are so inclined.

Not only that, but in your training, you will also have the opportunity to influence future doctors as you work with medical students and residents. If you can lead someone to Christ, or encourage Christians in training to keep their focus on God, think of the impact that is multiplied. They will hopefully, in turn, go and impact their communities and the people they have influence over.

Another strategic reason to be in medicine is the eternal impact you can have with your patients, as I alluded to in the previous chapter and in my personal statement.

The one blessing of becoming sick is that we become painfully aware of our mortality, how weak and small we are in ourselves in spite of what amazing things we have accomplished. It doesn't help that the hospital is a terrifying place for someone who is already feeling crappy and that the gowns are toilet-paper thin (and not the two-ply variety) and don't cover adequately all the necessary goods. It forces one to think about things like what's important in life, death, and God. These are topics we can conveniently and happily avoid when all is well and our bodies are doing what they're supposed to.

As a physician I have the deep honor of intersecting someone's life as those questions are starting to emerge. The doctor-patient relationship is special. Within minutes, complete strangers will share with me things they have never told anyone. I am invited not just to care for them physically, but also to come alongside them in their spiritual and emotional journeys. Of course there is a danger of abusing that vulnerability and imposing our worldviews and attitudes against the patient's will, so we need to take care not to do that.

But if the patient gives permission, it can be appropriate to share with patients our personal experiences with pain, our sources of strength, and the role faith plays in our life. There are studies that show patients actually want their physicians to ask them about their spiritual health. Some even would like their doctors to pray with them. Not only is spiritual care something that is appropriate because patients like it and it makes them feel better, but there is evidence that one's spirituality impacts a variety of disease processes.[18] In fact, JCAHO, an accrediting body for healthcare organizations, mandates that spiritual assessments be done on every patient. Questions similar to what they suggest asking include:[19]

"What are the patient's sources of strength?"

"Does prayer play a role in the patient's life?"

"What impact has the illness had on the patient and the family?"

The simple question of asking a patient's source of strength has opened up wonderful conversations about God and the role of faith in that person's life. It has led to praying with patients and family. This is not the same as forcing our beliefs on anyone. It doesn't happen with every patient at every encounter. It is by invitation. In fact, more often than not we are invited, but are too busy to notice. Those with interest in hospital-based medicine in particular can have tremendous opportunities to show the love of Christ during a time of crisis.

> God reminded her of her worth as a person, motivating her to care for her body. She reminded me that health extends beyond just physical healing.

But even if your patients do not openly invite you to care for them spiritually, you, as the physician, need to take the initiative at times. That's why there are JCAHO mandates because they recognize the need for spiritual care, regardless of whether patients think they need it or not. It's just good medicine. Providing spiritual care is no different than providing any other type of care. Not many people are fans of the prostate exam, but there are times when that procedure is necessary. Similarly, just because your patients don't feel comfortable talking about their sexual practices doesn't mean you don't and shouldn't ask about them. Your job as a physician is to identify the underlying needs in addition to addressing the patient's chief complaint in order to provide the best care.

Just as one will need to learn how to take a sexual history without giggling and blushing, one does not automatically know how to provide spiritual care without practice. There are organizations that do trainings to help students in medicine and health professionals integrate spiritual care, such as The Medical Strategic Network. During the summer after my first year of medical school, I attended their Whole Person Care Preceptorship.[20] It is a month-long program designed to teach Christian health students how to incorporate their faith in the practice of medicine.

The preceptorship includes seminars on practical skills such as how to take a spiritual history, how to share your faith respectfully, and how to pray with patients. You have the opportunity to shadow Christian providers and see how they interact with their patients. There is also a time for small group mentoring to discuss the integration of faith and practice and how to keep one's faith strong in the midst of training. For me, that was a really impactful time of building relationships and learning more about my calling in medicine. Shorter weekend trainings are scheduled throughout the year as well.

Medicine is such a diverse field that you really could do anything and it could be used to impact others for the kingdom. I speak mostly about how medicine can be used as a means to express God's love for the poor because that's how I have been convicted. I hope you don't get the impression that in order to be a good Christian doctor you have to forsake the specialties and embrace primary care. But if you do have that passion to work with the poor, check out the Christian Community Health Fellowship.[21] They are a group of Christian physicians dedicated to using healthcare to proclaim the gospel among the poor.

Again, it doesn't mean you have to work for a non-profit in order to be in God's will. I know graduates who work for private organizations who are improving the care and transition of care of the uninsured that show up at their doors. One private physician I know volunteers his time at free clinics and leads his church on medical mission trips on a regular basis. If you have an interest in a sub-specialty, there is a great need for medical education overseas to train native specialists. God can use you in any field, any setting.

The medical field opens up so many doors that the opportunities really are limited only by our imaginations. However, most of the time we are limited by how much we are willing to let God direct our steps. If you want to connect with Christian physicians and explore ways to use medicine to glorify God, I encourage you to look up the Christian Medical and Dental Associations.[22] Many medical schools have CMDA chapters or something similar.

They also hold joint school events that can be a source of networking and support. I served as a regional student representative for a term so there are leadership opportunities available nationally as well.

Medical professionals are able to bring comfort in a time of transparency and fear, caring not just for the physical. Unfortunately it does not come automatically, but it requires sensitivity to the Holy Spirit and willingness to be used by God in this way. It does take investment and an ongoing, vital personal relationship with God in order to be able to offer something that is real and not just another cliché.

*   *   *

With all that has been said, I hope I made the case that you should not pursue a career in medicine until you have made Jesus the Lord of your life, considered the ways in which you have been gifted, and counted the cost of what becoming a doctor entails. There are great costs, but there can be tremendous opportunities for eternal impact as long as it is Christ we are seeking to please. These opportunities for spiritual impact arise in every field of medicine.

If at the end of all this you have the privilege of being called into medicine, a more daunting challenge awaits: How can your convictions to serve God carry on beyond your training? For the rest of the book, I will offer some principles that have been helpful in maintaining the right perspective. My hope and prayer is that you will hold on to the calling that God has placed in your heart to be used for His glory throughout your vocational training.

Unfortunately, there have been many well-intentioned Christians who go into medicine with a big desire to serve God, but somewhere along the way get lulled into simply serving themselves. This is true not just in medicine, but in any field. Why is it that some people can have such strong desires to serve God initially but end up chasing the American Dream like everyone else? What are some things we can do now so when we actually become whatever it is we want to be, we will not just have the skills, but also the heart desire to carry out God's purposes?

Even if you don't choose to go into medicine, if you just want to be used in God's kingdom, these are principles that will be helpful in whatever career you pursue. So if you are ready for the next step, read on! My prayer is for you to hold fast to the Christ perspective, not just regarding your future endeavors, but in all of life.

Reflection Questions

1. At the end of your life, what will be most important to you? Does how you live now reflect those convictions?

2. What do you make of Jesus and the Bible's claims about Him? If you are a Christian, are you really living as His disciple? What role do you play in God's kingdom purposes?

3. How can any career be used to serve God? What has God specifically put on your heart to pursue?

Part II

Do You Still Want to Go Into Medicine?

Well done, good and faithful servant! You have been faithful with a few things; I will put you in charge of many things. Come and share your master's happiness! (Matthew 25:21).

Chapter 5

Obey the Obvious

I THINK EVERY COMMITTED CHRISTIAN LONGS TO HEAR the words of Matthew 25:21, "Well done, good and faithful servant!" when at last we meet our heavenly Master face to face. It definitely is preferable to Matthew 25:26, "You wicked, lazy servant!" We want to make sure we spend this life well, using wisely the talents God has entrusted to us, walking in His will.

A common question that comes up, though, is, "God, what is your will for my life?" The Bible unfortunately doesn't describe exactly how our lives are to unfold. But have you read that thing? It's huge! It tells us many things that we should be responding to. And maybe we have no right asking God for more if we aren't even paying attention to what He has already given us. It's like my twin nephew and niece asking me for more M&M's® while they are still holding some in their hands. Stop asking me until you finish yours or I won't give you any more. I might even eat the ones you do have.

It is true that there are things God is not clear about. He does not write out in the sky (usually) who you should marry, what college to go to, and what job to take. But there are a lot of things that God does spell out, and spells out clearly. You don't have to read very far in the Bible to find out that God cares about the Holy Spirit's work in our lives to make us like Christ, the process of sanctification (becoming more holy, sacred, or set apart for God).

In fact, one of the goals of a Christian is to be conformed to the image of Christ. Paul writes in Colossians 1:28-29 that he is spending his life trying to "present everyone perfect in Christ." God cares about our sanctification, and we have the Scriptures as a guide to what that sanctification looks like. Before we entertain grand plans of advancing God's kingdom, we need to start by obeying the obvious. We need to pay attention to what God has already made clear to us.

I have been in some sort of tutoring, academic club, or test prep program for as long as I can remember. There were English instructors, math tutors, SAT classes, and MCAT prep courses. Why? Because my parents knew that I wasn't going to get into medical school without intentional training. After college I endured eight years of study and hands-on training. In medical school, there were periods when I would literally spend the entire day hitting the books. There were weeks in residency where all I did was eat, sleep, and work. Patients weren't just going to entrust their lives into my hands because I wanted to be a doctor; I had to train.

It's like that with everything we want to become good at, whether recreation or vocation. We have to train, and we all understand that. Yet most Christians go about their spiritual lives expecting to automatically grow into godliness. Like osmosis, we'll just learn because we show up to church and carry our Bibles around. Obviously life doesn't work that way.

Granted, we do have the Holy Spirit working in us, and we do not have the ability to grow into Christ-likeness on our own strength. Different people may have poured into our lives, but ultimately any kind of growth is from God according to Paul (1 Corinthians 3:5-7). The same Paul, though, reminds us in Philippians 2:12-13 that God works in us while we work out our salvation. There is participation on our part. God perfects us as we walk in step with the Spirit, obeying what God has laid out for us through the Scriptures. It's like a dance where God leads and we follow. On occasion, He drags us along (or carries us, if you prefer the greeting card version).

First Samuel 15:22 says, "To obey is better than sacrifice, and to heed is better than the fat of rams." Thank goodness, we can put our fat away. God desires from us a heart that desires to obey His commands. This is not always the case, but most of the hard things in my life have been the consequences of choosing my own way over God's. Now those are the times I have learned the most and God does promise in Romans 8:28 that He sovereignly works together the good and the bad of our lives ultimately for the good of His children. While all that is wonderful, I do think there is a greater blessing in simple obedience, the first time around.

Do you want to be used in a big way when you are done with your schooling and training, whatever field you have chosen? Let's make sure to be doing the "small" things, what we know we ought to be doing so that God may entrust us with even greater. As Matthew 25:21 says, "You have been faithful with a few things; I will put you in charge of many things." So, what are these obvious things we should be obeying?

Read the Word

There are so many facets of obedience we can (and should) talk about, but I will only focus on a few areas. First, we need to read and study the Bible. Scripture is the living Word of God, the primary way in which God still speaks to us. If that's the case, we better be reading and studying the Bible if we are serious about doing God's will.

John 1:18 says, "No one has ever seen God, but God the One and Only, who is at the Father's side, has made him known." Jesus, through His incarnation, revealed God who is unseen. Jesus is the "image of the invisible God," as it says in Colossians 1:15. And how do we come to know Jesus, who He was, what He taught, what He was passionate about, and how He lived? By reading the Scriptures.

We need to cultivate a love for the Bible. It's great to have our fifteen minutes of devotional quiet time a day (if that), but that falls way short of the thirst we ought to have for the living Word of God. Joshua 1:8 says we are to meditate on the Scriptures day and night. In Psalm 19, the psalmist exalts the laws of God as more precious than gold and sweeter than honey. Jesus, quoting the Old Testament, says in Matthew 4:4, "Man does not live on bread alone, but on every word that comes from the mouth of God." Do we see God's Word as necessary to our soul as food is to our body? Or are our daily devotions merely a duty that needs to be checked off?

> Before we entertain grand plans of advancing God's kingdom, we need to start by obeying the obvious.

And beyond just reading the Word devotionally, we need to develop a habit of studying the Scriptures. "Blah, that's for the theologians, I don't need that for everyday living," you might say. Well, that's what I used to think until I started taking classes at Talbot. A theologian is simply a studier of God, so every Christian is a theologian of sorts. If you probe far enough, any sinful action can ultimately be traced back to bad theology, whether a faulty view of ourselves or of God. Wasn't Satan's first temptation a casting of doubt on what God really said (Genesis 3:1)?

If we do not want to be led astray by the many lies of the evil one and the false promises of this world, we must have a steady diet of the truth of God's Word.

Not everyone has the privilege of formal study of the Scriptures (although if you have the opportunity to take some seminary classes I highly recommend it), but we ought to routinely study the Word, whether with fellow Christians or alone. We have more resources at our disposal than ever before, so there's really no good excuse for not understanding the Bible. We need to learn how to properly interpret the text before we hastily apply it into our lives. Many start with trying to figure out what the Bible means to us, right now, and that is a very dangerous way to read the Bible. Not everything in Scripture is a direct promise to us, and Satan can use what we take out of context to weaken our faith in God and His Word.

We may have a master's degree, a medical degree, or even a doctor of philosophy (perhaps all three!), but what grade is our Bible knowledge? Psalm 119:105 says, "Your word is a lamp to my feet and a light for my path." Some of us are walking around holding our unlit lamps wondering why we can't make sense of our lives. Not that the Bible is a tell-me-what-decision-I-should-make-right-now magic eight ball. But we need to become familiar with all of Scripture (not just the New Testament!) to understand God's heart, what He has done throughout history, and how His salvation plan will unfold. The past informs the present, and gives us hope for the future. We need to understand how we fit into God's overarching story, rather than creating for ourselves a "god" we want to worship and the story we like to live in.

Pray

A word of caution is necessary here. As nerdy types who love to study, we have the temptation to study the Bible for the sake of more knowledge. The constant struggle I have when I'm studying for seminary is to remember the goal for which I am doing all of this: To love more and more God and my neighbor, and to become more like Christ. Growing in knowledge of God has to go hand in hand with a deepening relationship with God. It has to be accompanied by prayer.

Prayer is not just talking with God, but it is a way in which we attend to the Holy Spirit's work in our lives. That's why Paul commands us to "pray continually" in 1 Thessalonians 5:17. He doesn't mean we should sit all day and pray for this, that, and the other thing. But it is an exhortation to live in constant fellowship with God through the Holy Spirit who is always active in our lives and communing with the Father.

Without prayer, our quest for Bible knowledge will simply dry up the soul. That's why some call seminary a "spiritual cemetery." The intellectual life may blow up exponentially, but if the soul is not cultivated through prayer, pride will quickly come and quench the love in our hearts. The main way that God communicates with us is through the written Word, but we need prayer to discern how it applies in our lives.[23]

Prayer is going to be your life-line when you are in the thick of your training, consumed with the stress and pressures of preparing for your career. There were times after six-

teen hours straight of studying for the boards or trying to finish my work after being up for thirty hours so I can get out
of the hospital where I couldn't even remember why I was
doing all of this. There were mornings where I dreaded getting out of bed or times when I just wanted to scream if one
more patient told me his or her total body was in pain. You
need to be connected to God so you can be reminded of your
calling, and be strengthened to take it one step at a time.

Now, that is not to say that we pray simply when crisis
bangs on our door. The big cliché of Christianity is that it
is not a religion, but a relationship, right? Yet, for so many,
the only time we pray is when we need something. We
need to build the habit of coming before God, not just
when there's a crisis, but in the everydays of our lives. Relationships take work, and we'll unpack that a little more
in the next chapter. Can we really hear God's voice and
know His heart without spending time with Him in
prayer? I'm convinced that we will not be able to hear
God's prodding in the big things of our lives if we are not
aware of His voice in our day-to-day living. If you are having trouble staying awake while praying now in college or
medical school, wait until you get to residency.

Of course we can (and should) pray for things. Pastor
Francis Chan said in a sermon once something along the
lines of how there is nothing like the experience of answered
prayer. If our prayers are answered, that means the Almighty
God, the Creator of heaven and earth, heard us, and He acted.
The living God responded to us. That's the beauty of Christianity; that through Christ, we have access to the Creator God
who actually cares about what is going on in our lives.

Holiness

Even if you only read the Bible for fifteen minutes every day, you should pretty quickly realize that holiness is a big deal to God. And not just His holiness, but the holiness of His people as well. First Peter 1:14-16 says, "As obedient children, do not conform to the evil desires you had when you lived in ignorance. But just as he who called you is holy, so be holy in all you do; for it is written: 'Be holy, because I am holy.'" God expects His people to live according to the highest standard.

Many well-meaning Christians who want to read the Bible straight through usually take an early exit somewhere in Leviticus. Everything is pretty exciting up until two-thirds into Exodus where it starts describing in painstaking detail what the tabernacle, ark, and the priestly garments need to look like. And then we get into Leviticus and it's pretty much game over with descriptions of a zillion different sacrifices, rules, and regulations. Why do we need those books? Some of us might not even notice if someone took those sections away from our Bibles. Well, in part, these books paint a picture that you can't worship God any way you please. God is set apart from all the other idols so He gives His people these laws to live by to set them apart as well.

Throughout the Bible we find that God takes His holiness ultra seriously. God consumed Aaron's sons Nadab and Abihu with fire in Leviticus 10 because they offered up incense in a way that was not prescribed. God struck down Uzzah because he tried to keep the ark from falling to the ground by touching it with his hands in 2 Samuel 6. God ultimately judged Israel and brought them into exile because they defiled themselves with idolatry and sinful practices. Similar to how God called Israel to be His chosen people, 1 Peter 2:9 says that Christians "are a chosen people, a royal priesthood, a holy nation, a people belonging to God, that you may declare the praises of him who called you out of darkness into his wonderful light."

As the people of God commissioned to carry out His purposes, we must be holy as God is holy. As God's ambassadors into this world, we must reflect God not just in what we do, but in who we are. That means purifying our lives of what is not pleasing to God, and putting on what is. Part of the gospel message God wants to spread throughout the nations is in the transformed lives of the messengers. How do we figure out what is and isn't pleasing to God? It goes back to reading the Scriptures.

> We need to understand how we fit into God's overarching story, rather than creating for ourselves a "god" we want to worship and the story we like to live in.

Before we buckle down and tighten our bootstraps to get holy, we do have to remember, and keep on remembering, that the holiness God demands is nothing we can achieve on our own. The lesson of the Old Testament is that our own efforts can never fully satisfy the requirements of God's laws. This is where Jesus comes in yet again; through His death on the cross not only are all our sins forgiven, but through Jesus it is as if we have obeyed perfectly every command of God.

Through faith in Christ we are made holy in God's sight. Through the Holy Spirit's work and our participation, holiness eventually becomes an internal reality as previous sinful habits and attitudes are replaced by God's truth and righteous character. Of course this does not mean we need to be perfect in order to serve and be used by God. As a matter of fact, God uses us in our weakness to shame the wisdom of the world (1 Corinthians 1:27-30) and God's power is made perfect in our weaknesses (2 Corinthians 12:9).

But are you intentional about opening your weaknesses to God? Are you concerned about becoming more like Christ? Are you spending time reading the Bible to see what kind of people we ought to be? Are you in prayer asking the Holy Spirit to reveal areas of sin in your heart? Are you in community where people have freedom to speak into your life? Where you can find accountability on issues like sexual purity, which is another area God's Word is very clear on. As you are asking, "God, how do you want me to serve in Your kingdom?" will you also ask, "God, how can I grow to become more like Christ?"

Love

One of them, an expert in the law, tested him with this question: "Teacher, which is the greatest commandment in the Law?" Jesus replied: "'Love the

*Lord your God with all your heart and with all
your soul and with all your mind.' This is the first
and greatest commandment. And the second is
like it: 'Love your neighbor as yourself.' All the Law
and the Prophets hang on these two command-
ments"* (Matthew 22:35-40).

A goal of the Christian life is to become like Christ. You
can argue that these verses capture pretty much what that
looks like. Again, we could talk about so many different
ways that we ought to be obeying. We should be carrying
out the Great Commission, sharing our faith, and making
disciples. We should be helping the poor. We should be
putting off anger, and the list goes on and on. But, as Jesus
says, all the commands fall into place if we are loving God
and loving one another. And the Bible makes it clear, especially in the letters of John, that loving God involves
obeying God's command to love one another.

I won't repeat what I've already said about how we need
to experience the love of God in order to properly love
others. But I do want to remind you that whatever career
you end up choosing, if you want to do it for the Lord,
you'll need to do it out of a love for God and a love for people. Take away a love for people and your work just becomes a duty, an obligation to God because you are
supposed to do it. Like biblical knowledge without prayer,
this will dry up your soul. Absent the love of God and you
will quickly experience burnout and bitterness, and it'll be
a long time in recovery before you will dare to love again.

* * *

I should have prefaced this chapter with the disclaimer that I write this not as one who has perfected all these things, but as a fellow believer on the journey toward sanctification. It is a life goal to know the Word, to pray without ceasing, to be made holy inwardly as I am positionally before God, and to love as Jesus loves. But since we know this is exactly God's will for our lives, let's be intentional in growing in these areas while we wait on the Lord for the details.

After all, isn't this what a relationship with God looks like? Opening our hearts to God and being transformed by the Holy Spirit as we read the Bible, pray, and serve others in love? And we need to remain in relationship with God if we want to keep on doing kingdom work and not burn out. Let's be honest, doing God's work is hard, especially if it involves working with people.

But, if we are walking in step with the Spirit and living out our faith in love for one another, we have the promise that God will fill us up to continue to do His work. We have "streams of living water" in the Holy Spirit within us as it says in John 7:38. Isaiah 58:11 says the one who practices true religious acts "will be like a well-watered garden, like a spring whose waters never fail."[24] What a beautiful picture of God's sustaining love. If we continue to open our lives up to God through these spiritual disciplines, walking with the Spirit, God will continue to minister to us so that we have more than enough to pour out in service to others.

God desires simple obedience through faith. He told Abraham to go, and Abraham went. Jesus said follow, and the disciples followed. God sent Paul to the Gentiles, and he obeyed. Jonah didn't go in the direction God asked, and a fish ate him and took him there. I'm surprised we don't hear more about people swallowed whole by fish. I personally stay away from the ocean. It's terrifying.

Reflection Questions

1. How have you gone about trying to figure out God's will for your life?

2. What role does the Bible play in your life? Do you see it as the primary way in which God communicates with us? What has God clearly revealed in His Word that you are ignoring?

3. How is the balance between your discipline of prayer and Bible reading? How can prayer become a bigger part of your life?

Chapter 6

Water
the Grass

"THE GRASS IS ALWAYS GREENER . . . WHERE YOU WATER it." This is my favorite quote from Dr. Nick. This chapter is a summary of the most important lessons I have learned from him as I've listened to his talks and spent time with him. I'm getting ahead of myself, but if you don't have a mentor who can guide you in doing what you wish to be doing in the future, make finding one a priority.

If God has placed a strong conviction in your heart to serve Him in a particular way "when you grow up," it is really easy to think:

Hey, I am just a student now. When I graduate, then I can have the freedom to pursue what God has in store for me.

When I finish my studies, then I'll have the skills to get involved with that kind of ministry.

You know, I need to get more established at work before focusing on why God called me to this job in the first place.

Even when it comes to our spiritual walk, we can fall into the trap of thinking, *When I get to spring break or summer break, then I'll have time to read the Bible and pray so I can figure out God's calling for me.* We need to be very careful because the habits we develop now will be the habits we live with when the future becomes the present. As much as we want to, we will not be able to flip on a switch and all of a sudden be the people we need to be when the "time" finally comes to serve God. The grass may be greener on the other side, but you don't own that grass. And it probably got that green because the owner took care of it, invested time in it, and made sure to water it.

We really are creatures of habit. I sit in the same seat in class and at church every week, take the same routes to work every day, and eat my chicken nuggets the same way every time. I eat all the skin first, and then finish the rest with sweet and sour sauce, yum! I used to lick clean all of the sweet and sour sauce after the nuggets were gone, but that's one habit I fortunately broke.

Who you are today is the result of habits you developed as you grew up, and how you live now will very much set the pattern for how you will live in the future. Is prayer not a priority now? It probably won't be a priority in the future. Is evangelizing not a part of your life now? It probably won't be a part of your life in the future. Is church not on your schedule right now? It probably still won't be in the future, unless you are very intentional about making the choices now to embrace those things and change old habits.

At the beginning of medical school there were Christians who wanted to use their gifts for God. But when the studying started and the hours got crazy, many stopped coming out to our weekly fellowship meetings, and some quit church altogether. I understand there are times when school or work gets really overwhelming, and sometimes you just need the extra couple of hours to study or finish a project or paper, or even just to sleep. But by continually prioritizing other things over God, before you know it, you really aren't walking with the Lord anymore.

Most Christian medical fellowships I know of are organized and attended by the first- and second-year students. When third year rolled around, people disappeared off to their different rotations. Some resurfaced during their fourth year, but not nearly the number that came out during their first and second years. I don't want to presume on anyone's salvation or relationship with God, but my experience in ministry has been that those who don't stay in fellowship with the body of believers typically don't do well.

Medical school is hard, no doubt about it. There will be times when we will not be able to do all we want to do, or know we should do. I hate to say this, but as hard as medical school is, residency is on a completely different level. Not only is residency physically and intellectually taxing, but you also have the added emotional burden of caring for real-life people. If you didn't have time for God

in medical school, then forget about having any relationship with God in residency. The work hour laws are different now so people aren't in the hospital for a hundred-plus
hours a week, but even then there's no comparison. If your
spiritual disciplines were not in place before residency
started, there is no way you will suddenly develop them.

A fellow brother and I started a Bible study for Christian residents during our intern year. Trying to organize
a time to meet when everyone had a different monthly
call schedule was a logistical nightmare. We had a few reg-
ulars and people would pop in and out, but if you weren't
already convicted to stay in fellowship with other believers, there were way too many other things that you could
do instead.

That brother went on to complete his residency in
emergency medicine at a different hospital where he continued to hold Bible studies. After spending some time in
France for language study, he is now in Africa doing medical missions, fulfilling a conviction he received in medical
school. He made the choices to put God first, every step
of the way, and it shows by the life he's living now. He is
an inspiration; I miss him but am excited to see how God
will use him and his team overseas.[25]

Another resident who participated regularly felt God
call him and his wife to eventually care for orphans overseas. What did he do to explore that calling? He set aside
vacation time during residency to go on a vision trip to
India with his wife, working with the local orphanages.
They also certified to become foster parents, and in the
middle of residency, they took care of a little girl needing

placement for a time. (Amazing, right?) Every time I meet up with them I am reminded that we live for more than just our own comforts, and I am encouraged to continue seeking first God's will. We need to surround ourselves with kingdom-minded people like these.

I don't think life ever gets any less busy. Sure, in college there is less school time and more freedom, but there is also more stuff to fill your time with. After you get into the working world, you'll realize how much more time you had in college when you could ditch a class whenever you felt like it. Yes, post-residency life is great, but now I have a relationship with my wife to cultivate and church ministry duties to fulfill. There's still only twenty-four hours in a day and somehow those hours just get filled up.

> Who you are today is the result of habits you developed as you grew up, and how you live now will very much set the pattern for how you will live in the future.

I can't imagine what life will be like when kids come into the picture. I want to be a dad, but I'm terrified because it means saying good-bye to life as I know it. The things we don't prioritize now will be the same things we won't prioritize in the future. My backyard and my piano skills (or lack thereof) testify to that. It's the basic principle of sowing and reaping.

If we have not put in the effort to sow godly character and habits, there will be nothing to reap when the time comes. I confess that when I finally had days off during medical school and residency, praying and reading the Bible were not on top of my to-do list. No, I vegged my brains out, blowing through whole seasons of television shows and countless movies. Not that we can't have fun and relax, but we need more than just recreation to power our Christian service. We need to be intentional about filling ourselves with God so that we can continue to pour out. That's why they are called spiritual disciplines, not spiritual automatics.

Relationships Take Work

A great joy in being part of youth ministry is seeing those kids you have invested in make good choices and do well in their spiritual walks as they go through college and beyond. But there is also the pain of hearing about those who used to be part of the church, but are not walking with God anymore. Taking a step back, it's the same principle when it comes to growing in our relationship with the Lord. Consider this passage in John:

> *I am the true vine, and my Father is the gardener. He cuts off every branch in me that bears no fruit, while every branch that does bear fruit he prunes so that it will be even more fruitful. You are already clean because of the word I have spoken to you. Remain in me, and I will remain in you. No branch can bear fruit by itself; it must remain in the vine. Neither can you bear fruit unless you remain in me.*

I am the vine; you are the branches. If a man re-
mains in me and I in him, he will bear much fruit;
apart from me you can do nothing. If anyone does
not remain in me, he is like a branch that is thrown
away and withers; such branches are picked up,
thrown into the fire and burned (John 15:1-6).

This passage illustrates that to maintain a vital, growing spiritual life, we need to remain in fellowship with Jesus. Our relationship with Jesus is no different from any other: we need to invest. During my intern year while Priscilla and I were still dating, she had serious doubts whether or not our relationship could work. There were many days where I would be completely exhausted after work, too tired to spend time together. And even if we had time together, I was so detached from what I was feeling I couldn't engage in any meaningful connection. She felt like she was dating a robot; I kind of felt like one.

It wasn't like I was trying to not have a relationship with her, but I had to stuff a lot away just to be able to get up the next day and do it all over again. So maintaining a relationship is not only about having time together. Just because Priscilla and I see each other every day now doesn't mean we automatically have a real relationship. We have to choose to connect and open ourselves to one another. We have date nights once a week and I try my hardest to protect at least that time to intentionally engage and build our relationship. It's the same with God; we have to be diligent in carving out time for Him. We need to be in the practice of opening our hearts to Christ in us through the Holy Spirit. Unfortunately it is much easier to pop in a movie, play some video games, or simply just sleep.

While, again, there is nothing we can do to bring about our own salvation or sanctification, a true relationship with God requires surrendering to Jesus and attending to the Holy Spirit. The decision is ours to open up to Jesus and remain in relationship. That's where the spiritual disciplines come in, not as a means of changing ourselves, but as a way to position our hearts for the sanctifying work of the Holy Spirit.

Most people do not wake up one day and all of a sudden decide, "No, I really don't believe in God," and renounce their faith. Rather, it is the continual choosing of ourselves over God and the things of God that causes our hearts to harden to a point where one day God feels distant, and we wonder why in the world we believed all this "Christian stuff" in the first place.

Fuel the Fire

In 2 Timothy 1:6 Paul tells Timothy, who was commissioned to faithfully preach the Word, to "fan into flame the gift of God." There is truth in the statement, "If you don't use it, you'll lose it," and it doesn't just apply to your muscles. If God has placed a conviction on your heart, a particular way in which to use your gifting, you need to continue fanning that into flame.

Do you have a burden for missions? Try to go on a short-term trip, attend missions conferences, and hang out with missionaries. Practice sharing your faith and talking with people about God. Try foods you don't usually eat. Do you feel called to teach? Start by helping out with the elementary or junior high ministry at church.

You want to provide spiritual care to your patients? The best time to start is as a medical student, since you get so much time to spend with patients. Learn how to take spiritual histories as a student and how to pray with your patients.

You want to live for others and not yourself? You can start that while you are in school through your study habits. I disliked study groups because they are more like "talking until midnight and then we really have to study" groups. It was much more efficient studying on my own. I was great at taking care of myself, but in retrospect I missed out on a lot of relationship building and opportunities to minister in times of vulnerability that only comes out late at night under significant duress. Remember that the Great Commission is not just obeyed in some distant land by "professional" Christians. All believers are to share the love of Christ and make disciples right where they are, whatever their season of life.

If there is a Christian medical fellowship at your school, make an effort to join. It's not realistic to attend every week, but it's helpful to be around people who are not freaking out about studying all the time. It's so easy to be caught up with what people around you are caught up with. Surround yourself with people who are kingdom-minded, who can remind you of what God has called you to. They will also be a source of support that your non-medical Christian friends may not be able to provide since

they can't relate to what you are going through. Even if
you can find just one other dedicated brother or sister in
medicine with whom you can meet regularly to pray and
study the Word together, that can make a huge difference
on how you come out of training.

Stewardship

There were some people in the Bible who were audibly
called and set apart for a specific task: Abraham, the disciples, and Paul come to mind. God may have called you
undeniably to pursue medicine, or some other field. If
that's the case, you better pursue it! Others, though, were
simply living in obedience to whatever they were doing
at the moment and God quietly directed their steps. Part
of watering the grass (and obeying the obvious) is being
a good steward of what you have been entrusted with,
faithfully serving in your current capacity.

There are many examples of individuals who were
faithfully serving when God called them to a greater task.

> The things we
> don't prioritize now
> will be the same
> things we won't
> prioritize in
> the future.

Consider David, who was
just doing his job as a
shepherd, carrying out his
duties of protecting his
sheep from bears and
lions. When Samuel came
into town, David wasn't
even around because he
was in the fields. God

used those experiences to deepen David's trust in God, strengthening David to fight against Goliath (1 Samuel 17:34-37). Or consider Timothy, who, by faithfully serving in Lystra, caught the eye of Paul who ended up taking him along on his missionary journeys (Acts 16:1-3).

There's also the unnamed guy in 2 Corinthians who Paul sent with Titus to carry out his collection for the Jerusalem poor. This is what Scripture says about him: "And we are sending along with [Titus] the brother who is praised by all the churches for his service to the gospel. What is more, he was chosen by the churches to accompany us as we carry the offering, which we administer in order to honor the Lord himself and to show our eagerness to help" (2 Corinthians 8:18-19).

This guy doesn't even get named, but he came highly recommended by the churches he worked with. He had the privilege of participating with Paul and Titus in the ministry to the Jerusalem saints because he was faithful in his service, whatever he was doing. He made it into the Bible too, which is pretty cool. What areas of ministry has God allowed you to participate in? Who has God placed in your life to love on and minister to?

Even as you are going through your training, whatever phase you are in, preparing for whatever profession, don't neglect what you have been entrusted with. Don't think you can wait until you are done with school, or that you can wait for a "better" time. If God has given you something now, now is the better time. We want to be faithful with what God has given to us so He can entrust us with even greater.

* * *

"AHHH, Jack," you protest. "This is so much stuff that I'm stressed out even thinking about how to incorporate all these things." Of course I am not saying you should take care of everyone else at the expense of your own grades and self-care. Obviously you will not be too helpful if you fail out of medical school (unless God has another plan for you, in which case that might actually be a blessing in disguise).

There is, for sure, the danger of over-extending yourself so this goes back again to prayer. We need to pray for wisdom about our own boundaries. I do bank on the fact that most people err on the side of self-preservation anyway, so I feel okay pushing the envelope a little bit. But if you know in your heart of hearts you struggle with people-pleasing and it's very difficult to say no, please take what I say with at least a tablespoon of salt.

We need to make God a priority in our lives now if we want to be used for His purposes in the future. It goes back to counting the cost and coming to a decision that Jesus is worth more than anything else in your life. There will always be plenty of temptations and excuses to put off service for God:

"Let's save up a little more money; you'll never know if something will happen."

"You worked so hard, you need some time to enjoy yourself. God understands."

"Was that really God calling me to work with the poor? God must have provided this job that pays more."

These excuses will sound really convincing if you haven't been in the habit of choosing God over yourself. Take every opportunity to choose God and to use the gifts God has given you. Don't neglect ministries you have the opportunity to get involved in while looking forward to potential greater ministry opportunities in the future. If you keep putting off God, you might find when the time comes to use your gifts to serve Him, the gifts might no longer be there, or you won't really care to use them. Of course you want to make sure you are building a strong technical foundation for whatever field you are entering during your training. Just make sure your spiritual foundation is as solid, if not more.

Reflection Questions

1. How much of your present character and habits are the result of your daily choices from the time you were growing up? How would you like things to be different, and what changes would you have to make now to achieve that?

2. In what ways can you start exploring what God has placed on your heart to pursue?

3. What gifts has God given you to build up His kingdom? What ministry opportunities do you have now to exercise those gifts?

Chapter 7

Humble Pie, Delicious!

Humility is one of those qualities you never seem to arrive at, because the moment you think you've got it, you probably don't. Pride is such a devious thing and Satan for sure knows how to take advantage of it to make us fall so we need to be on guard. Many have started their careers centered on God only to have their pride hijack their good intentions and make their careers all about themselves.

Those who make it into medical school and beyond certainly have a lot to be proud of. But no one likes a prideful doctor. Many of us probably have had the experience of meeting those physicians who walk around like gods among men. In truth, some of them do God-like things, holding people's lives in their hands and even bringing people back to life on occasion. Unfortunately, this attitude can start brewing in budding medical students.

This is an area where a Christian physician (or Christian anything) should be different. We take our lead from Jesus, who, as God in the flesh, ought to have been served, but came instead to serve those who were not even worthy to untie His sandals. Because Jesus emptied Himself for our sake, God exalted Him to the highest place with the greatest honor, before whom all knees will bow (Philippians 2:6-11). Consider Jesus' purpose in coming to this earth:

> *Jesus called them together and said, "You know that those who are regarded as rulers of the Gentiles lord it over them, and their high officials exercise authority over them. Not so with you. Instead, whoever wants to become great among you must be your servant, and whoever wants to be first must be slave of all. For even the Son of Man did not come to be served, but to serve, and to give his life as a ransom for many" (Mark 10:42-45).*

This great reversal is a theme woven throughout the Scriptures, from Jacob repeatedly getting the upper hand over Esau to the End Times when the wisdom of the world will be shamed by what mankind thought was foolishness on the cross. The Jews missed the Messiah—Jesus—because He didn't fit their picture. Recall that the Jewish nation was chosen by God to be His people to proclaim Him to all the surrounding nations. In the Old Testament we see God's special covenant relationship with the Israelites when He gave them His commands and dwelled among them.

At one point in history, the nation of Israel had great influence. They inherited the land promised to Abraham and eventually became a prominent power under King David and King Solomon. They had wealth and military strength, and many nations traveled to the temple to seek wisdom and to worship God. But because Israel repeatedly disregarded God's Law and ignored His prophets' warnings, God judged the nation and sent the people into exile. Because of His unfailing love and His covenantal promise, God eventually allowed a remnant to return to their land and start rebuilding the temple. But they would remain under the rule of foreign powers.

The Israelites had everything taken away from them, but God did not leave them without hope. He promised that one day, from the line of David, the Messiah would come to reign on the throne forever. Like Moses, who led Israel out of captivity under the Egyptians, the Messiah would rescue God's people. They would again

> If you keep putting off God, you might find when the time comes to use your gifts to serve Him . . . you won't really care.

have their own land, kingdom, and, more importantly, the presence of God.

Hundreds of years passed and world powers came and went, but the Jews still held out hope that God would be true to His word. You can imagine the excitement when they heard about someone who was healing the sick and driving out demons. He even raised the dead and claimed to be the Son of God. There was much hype about this Jesus guy, with thousands upon thousands following after Him, eager for His teachings and miracles. But then this Jesus started teaching weird things, something about eating His body and drinking His blood. He ended His career by being arrested. He was beaten and humiliated. To top it off He was executed for the world to see, suffering a disgraceful death while hanging on a cross (which, according to Deuteronomy 21:23, would mean He was cursed by God so all the more reason to reject Jesus).

The crowds deserted Jesus as quickly as they gathered, thinking He was just another false prophet who couldn't back up His claims. How could He have been the One? The Messiah was supposed to come in power. Like Gideon, Samson, or David, He was supposed to mobilize the Jewish people and overthrow the oppressive Roman government. Israel was supposed to get its land and wealth back, all that the people enjoyed under the reign of the glorious kings of old.

Little did they know that Jesus did come to usher in a kingdom, but not an earthly one. At least not yet. He didn't come to restore Israel to its former glory. Jesus came first to usher in the eternal kingdom of God. The people didn't understand that their relationship with God could not be restored yet because of their sin. The problem of sin had to be dealt with first before they could enter into God's kingdom, so Jesus came to deal with the sins of the world. He stepped down from glory in order to become the sacrifice needed to atone for the sins of all people throughout all time.

And Jesus didn't just have Israel in mind; He wanted the whole world to be reconciled to God. The Bible tells us that one day Jesus will come in power with the angels and God's kingdom will be established with every enemy force crushed under Jesus' feet. But first, God wants to redeem His people. As Mark 10:45 says, Jesus didn't come to be served, even though we are not even worthy to serve Him. No, Jesus came to serve, to empty Himself so that the world could be saved.

We are called to adopt the same attitude as Jesus, that our lives here would be emptied for the sake of others. While those of the world might pursue medicine for money and self-glory, as Christians, our calling is to consider others better than ourselves, and that includes the patients we are caring for. We are to use medicine not to further our own glory, but as a means to glorify God and point others to Him.

But it's so hard not to seek after our own glory, isn't it? There's a deep need in our hearts for significance because we were created for eternity. That need can only be filled through union with Christ, but apart from God, we grasp at every opportunity for self-glorification. And don't think just because we have good intentions we'll be immune. I started this book project thinking, *I just want to be helpful and give glory to God*. It didn't take very long for the evil one to whisper sweet nothings of grandeur into my ears, getting me thinking about the money and fame I could get from this. *New York Times* Bestseller list here I come! Never mind that I've written squat in the past. I probably shouldn't quit my day job just yet. I suppose if Satan can't get us to stop doing God's work, he'll get us to do it for the wrong reasons.

Humility is going to be a constant challenge in any career that requires knowledge and skills. The better you get at something, the more you are going to be tempted to take pride in what you do. We need to remind ourselves that, as Christians, we are called to serve others as Christ served us. Christ, who deserved all glory, respect, and honor, was the one who washed the disciples' feet. Jesus stepped down from majesty where He enjoyed perfect intimacy and fellowship with God the Father and the Holy Spirit to become a man to die on the cross for our sins.

We need to also remember that all our talents and abilities have their source in God Himself, who created us and gave us our gifts. Becoming a physician is a tremendous accomplishment, but it is only possible because of God's grace in our lives. We could easily be in a situation where it would be impossible to accomplish this goal no matter how hard we tried. When I first started working with the homeless population, I was shocked at how many people I met who had college degrees, and even graduate degrees. My presumptuous stereotypes were quickly shattered listening to some of their stories. Many had led normal, everyday working lives, but had lost it all to circumstances beyond their control. Not all homelessness is the result of drugs, alcohol, and whatever else we typically think of. Let's also not forget that billions of people live on less than two dollars a day, and not by choice. You did not get to choose where you were born because of your great talents and gifts.

Moses warned the Israelites before they crossed into the Promised Land:

> When the Lord your God brings you into the land he swore to your fathers, to Abraham, Isaac, and Jacob, to give you—a land with large, flourishing cities you did not build, houses filled with all kinds of good things you did not provide, wells you did not dig, and vineyards and olive groves you did not plant—then when you eat and are satisfied, be careful that you do not forget the Lord, who brought you out of Egypt, out of the land of slavery (Deuteronomy 6:10-12).

Prosperity is sometimes harder to handle than adversity. When times are difficult, it's much easier to keep God in mind, whether we are complaining or seeking His help. But when the good times are rolling, we have such a tendency to forget the work of God in our lives and easily think we were responsible for our own successes. It's easy to forget the many desperate prayers you sent God's way before the MCAT, anatomy exams, and every other time you were in trouble, after the fact.

Scrotums and Sin

We don't just need humility to be a good doctor. We need humility to not fall into spiritual complacency and, in some cases, spiritual death. It is so easy for us to go on auto-pilot in our spiritual lives and think everything is great. We can be so blinded to sin and to our apathy of sin. Our power to deny problems and make excuses is amazing.

I was working in the ER one time and this guy came in for abdominal pain. I did the standard history, getting all the gory details. Then I went to do an exam. Heart sounds were good, no murmurs. Lungs, pretty clear. Abdomen feels okay . . . wait, I feel a mass? Is this stool in his intestines? So I follow it and it's no stool. It goes down into his pants and there I find that his scrotum is the size of a grapefruit. I hope he didn't see me go bug-eyed.

> If Satan can't get us to stop doing God's work, he'll get us to do it for the wrong reasons.

I asked him how long he's had this and he told me four months. Four months? Are you kidding me? I asked him why he didn't come in earlier. He simply shrugged. I found out later he had a cancer of his testicle and it had spread all the way into his belly.

We might find that story incredulous. Why did he wait that long to come in? You would think if your scrotum was the size of a tennis ball that would raise some red flags. But if we are really honest, that's us, spiritually. Many of us live with cancers of sin growing in our lives little by little, but because of our pride we just go on ignoring it. Our pride deceives us into thinking we are hunky dory with the Lord. We need a humble heart to come before God regularly to ask the Holy Spirit to search our souls for what needs to be conformed into the image of Christ.

To give my patient credit, he was uninsured and didn't have access to regular medical care. If I was faced with a decision to fork up money to see a doctor or put food on the table, I wouldn't go to the doctor, either. That breaks my heart. This is just one small example of the injustices that exist in our medical system. So he wasn't just ignoring the problem, although part of it was thinking it was "no big deal." But we don't have that excuse. We have access to God every moment and God desires that we come to Him. We need to cultivate a humility about ourselves so that we are not blinded to the evil that is growing within.

Humility isn't just seeking after God, it's also looking to God's people for help and support. I will talk in the next chapter about how being in medicine really trains us to trust in ourselves instead of God and the church body, to our peril. As someone who has grown up serving in different ministries and now has a career of helping people, it is so hard to be on the receiving end. In this journey, not just in medicine, but in life, we need the encouragement of fellow brothers and sisters in Christ to keep us on the right path toward the prize.

But this is particularly true in medicine, which will demand of you one hundred percent and more. You will be

exposed to things, whether firsthand or from your patients' sharing, that will be traumatizing. Participating in
the still-born delivery of twins in their twenty-some weeks
of life comes to mind. Our tendency will be to tighten up
our scrubs and press on. "We need to be strong," we tell
ourselves. But emotions that are suppressed will eat away
at our souls if we are not careful. We need humility to realize when we are in trouble and be able to cry out for help,
and sometimes that involves professional counseling.
There is no shame in seeking out help.

We have such a strong aversion to weakness, which deceives us into thinking we can handle everything by ourselves. The world says you are strong if you can tough it
out and overcome difficulties by your willpower, that it is
embarrassing to need others and come off as weak and incapable. But that's the pride of our hearts speaking, the
rebellion in us that says we can be our own gods. The Bible
paints a strikingly different picture of strength. It is a picture of Jesus, a helpless babe, laid in a manger and utterly
dependent on His human parents. It is only in our weakness that we truly experience strength, because it is when
we come to the end of ourselves that we start to see we
were created to live in union with God and in dependence
on the Holy Spirit. Paul writes:

> To keep me from becoming conceited because of
> these surpassingly great revelations, there was
> given me a thorn in my flesh, a messenger of Satan,
> to torment me. Three times I pleaded with the Lord
> to take it away from me. But he said to me, "My

grace is sufficient for you, for my power is made perfect in weakness." Therefore I will boast all the more gladly about my weaknesses, so that Christ's power may rest on me. That is why, for Christ's sake, I delight in weaknesses, in insults, in hardships, in persecutions, in difficulties. For when I am weak, then I am strong (2 Corinthians 12:7-10).

Here is Paul, a mighty warrior for the Lord. He brought the gospel throughout much of the known world at the time, and in the process was stoned, flogged, arrested, and shipwrecked. If anyone was strong in his own ability and accomplishments, it would be him. Yet Paul recognized the source of his strength, and that it was actually in his weakness that he was made strong. It was in his weakness that he experienced the incredible power and grace of God.

It will be in our weakness that we will truly come to know God as well. We have to get rid of all our pretense that everything is just fine and realize that we need Jesus, not just for our salvation, but to live from day-to-day. But we in the medical field are good at pretending, aren't we? Residency is a giant exercise in pretending that we know what we are doing until we actually learn how. We will connect more deeply with God in our weakness, and it will make us better doctors. We will find a deeper connection with our patients as well because they are bringing us their weaknesses.

I don't mean to complicate the picture even more, but we do need to watch out for false humility. As I went through the process I really didn't like to talk about my medical school experience. I saw it as complaining and even prideful to draw so much attention to myself. I thought I was being humble by just chugging along, not making a scene. What I realized was that was actually pride. (So tricky!) I didn't want to seem weak, needing help and support. I wanted to put up this image of "Med school? Pshaw, no big deal. I'm just doing my thing, nothing to see here."

Now, there are ways to talk about medical school that are pride-driven: giving your opinion on every medically related topic as fact; putting down other people's hardships because it doesn't compare to medical school; bringing everything back to how hard medical school is, to name just a few. It happens even with the best of intentions. Be careful you are not taking pride in your apparent humility.

*   *   *

Just to give you a heads up, if you don't learn humility, you are going to be in for a reality check when you start your rotations in medical school, and for sure, during residency. It doesn't matter if you were the smartest person in the class all throughout high school, college, and medical school. The moment you step onto the hospital floor, you will feel like the dumbest person there (unless there are other medical students around). Unfortunately, book knowledge doesn't translate automatically into application in real life.

You will find that patients didn't read the textbook before coming in. They don't come in with multiple choice questions on their chests, either. At some point I knew all the muscles in the body and where they attached, memorized all the known antibiotics and their mechanism of action, and countless of other facts. But when I got my first page while on call because a patient had pain, I couldn't recall how much Tylenol® I could give and how to order it. Thank goodness for the Internet and nice nurses.

To remain humble despite the many obstacles you have overcome and the many accomplishments that are in store is a tremendously difficult task. But it is an essential one if we want to be used by God in a meaningful way. And not just that, the ultimate decision to reject God lies in the issue of pride. The Christian walk is a daily dying to your own pride, how you want your life to be. It is a question of who is in charge of your life: God or you.

This world loves the places of honor, recognitions, and the titles. We seek the MDs, JDs, PhDs, and even in ministry, the MAs, MDivs, ThMs, and even DMins. Of course we want to use these for the Lord, but we can get so busy collecting the titles we forget the purpose of all our gifts and accomplishments: to serve one another in the love and humility of Christ.

Professor, pastor, and author Tony Campolo often gave this challenge: Would you rather have titles or testimonies? When you die, would you like worldly titles decorating your tombstone? Or would you rather have people after people sharing testimonies of how God used you to impact His kingdom. I want to be happy if at the end of my life, people will simply say I was a faithful servant of others in the name of Christ. I certainly want to hear that from God when I see Him face to face.

Humble pie? Yes, please.

Reflection Questions

1. What personal accomplishments are you most proud of? Did those lead to more or less dependence on God and others?

2. What is your attitude toward your weaknesses? Is it easy to ask others for help?

3. What would it look like to serve your patients with the humility of Christ?

Chapter 8

You
Complete Me

I T's ALWAYS SAD TO HEAR ABOUT SOMEONE WHO WAS part of the youth group while growing up, but is no longer walking with God. I remember being at our church retreat some years ago talking to another leader about this. We wanted to know why this happened, and why even students who seemed on fire for the Lord ended up giving up on their faith.

We came up with theories about how people's everyday choices of self over God eventually can result in a hardened heart, or how unconfessed sins can hinder our intimacy with God. But what we thought was the number one reason was that those who ended up rejecting God were those who did not make church community a priority in their lives.

Now, whether or not those who once considered themselves Christians who "fell away" were really believers to begin with I'll leave for Bible scholars and Christian sleepovers. Obviously we were not experts on conversion and Christian growth, and I am not one now. But from being in youth ministry for the past ten years, this is an observation that has held true: Those who have a vibrant spiritual life have a vibrant Christian community life. We can't experience all of who God is by ourselves.

You might be thinking: *Wait a second, I thought all I need is God. My relationship with God is my own and no one else's business.* I would like to suggest that we cannot remain in Jesus and connect fully with God without the community of believers, God's church. And I say this even though by nature I am an introvert and can be quite content on my own.

No Man is an Island

In Genesis we find the account of God creating the world. God created some stuff and it was good, created some more stuff and that was also good. Then He created man and everything was very good. In Genesis 2 God looked at creation and He noticed Adam was by himself and concluded in Genesis 2:18, "It is *not* good for the man to be alone" (emphasis added).

Take a moment and think about that. This is an amazing verse. Recognize that the fall hadn't happened yet. Here, before sin had even entered the world and Adam had perfect fellowship with God, God declared it was not good that Adam had no fellowship, no community, and no connection with another human being. This also speaks to the importance and sacredness of the marriage relationship, but that is another book.

We are wired to connect not just with God, but also with God's people. There's a reason why solitary confinement is a form of punishment and torture. And the way God has arranged it, we actually connect more with God, come to experience God more fully through connecting with His people, the church. Why? I think in part because our God who created us is a community God. Let's look again to Paul:

> *For this reason I kneel before the Father, from whom his whole family in heaven and on earth derives its name. I pray that out of his glorious riches he may strengthen you with power through his Spirit in your inner being, so that Christ may dwell in your hearts through faith. And I pray that you, being rooted and established in love, may have power, together with all the saints, to grasp how wide and long and high and deep is the love of Christ, and to know this love that surpasses knowledge—that you may be filled to the measure of all the fullness of God.*

Now to him who is able to do immeasurably more than all we ask or imagine, according to his power that is at work within us, to him be glory in the church and in Christ Jesus throughout all generations, for ever and ever! Amen (Ephesians 3:14-21).

Paul has just spent the first two chapters of Ephesians describing the amazing love that God lavished on us through Christ and His death on the cross. He has explained how all of us were once separated from God, who is holy and pure, because of our sin. Since God is also just, He had to punish sin so His wrath was in store for us. But because God is also love, He sent His son, who lived a perfect life, to die on the cross, and His death paid for the sins in our place. Through faith in what Jesus had done, our relationship with God could be restored. That's the gospel, the good news of God.

> Those who have a vibrant spiritual life have a vibrant Christian community life. We can't experience all of who God is by ourselves.

Now that the Jews and Gentiles were reconciled together to God, Paul prayed for this united people that they would grow together into all the fullness of God. He asked God to grant His believers power through the Holy Spirit to turn their hearts to Him and to enable their hearts to embrace God through faith in Jesus Christ.

In this passage we see all three Persons of the Godhead at work in this wonderful work of salvation: God the Father, the Holy Spirit, and Jesus the Son. Each has His own role, existing in perfect intimacy and unity. And we are invited into that intimacy through faith in Christ and the indwelling of the Holy Spirit.

Our God is a community God. We might not understand completely the doctrine of the Trinity, but if we are believers, then we have experienced the Trinity working in our lives as we have come to faith. Just as God is a community God, we, His creation, are a community people. Paul prayed that the believers would *together* have power to understand more and more Christ's love so they may be filled by the fullness of God. According to Paul, this process of attaining totally all that God has in store for us happens in the context of community, "together with all the saints."

While it is true that God loves us individually, Scripture is clear that Jesus died so that a people, otherwise known as the church, would be set aside for God. In Ephesians 2:19-22, Paul talked about how the Jews and Gentiles in Christ were all of the same citizenship in God's household, and that together they were being built up to be a dwelling place of God. Paul went on in Ephesians 4:7-14 to describe how all believers were given gifts in order to "prepare God's people for works of service, so that the body of Christ may be built up until we all reach unity in the faith and in the knowledge of the Son of God and become mature, attaining to the whole measure of the fullness of God." We get a fuller sense of God and what He is like when everyone is serving together building up the church.

In between these two passages, we find a doxology praising God for His immeasurable power available to us and giving God glory. The apostle wrote, "to him be glory in the church *and* in Christ Jesus" (Ephesians 3:21, emphasis added). Here's another incredible verse. That God would receive glory through Christ Jesus makes sense. Jesus is the exact representation of God. He, in obedience, submitted to God's will, laying down His life. God is glorified completely through Jesus Christ. But Paul said that God's glory is to be represented in the church as well. Really? The church is to continue to do what Jesus did when He was on earth? If we are not careful, we can so easily gloss over the significance of those few words.[26]

We have to remember that the glory of God is a big deal. The Bible is essentially about God revealing His glory, ultimately through His Son, so all the earth can praise Him. And yet, according to Paul, the church is to be a vehicle to display the glory of God. We are to be like Jesus in bringing glory to God among the nations. Talk about a high calling. That's how serious God is about His church, the community of believers for whom Jesus died.

If that is the case, if God really entrusted the church with this critical task, it's no wonder Satan is doing so much trying to destroy the institution of the church. Looking around, we have to admit that Satan has done a pretty good job with all the news about corrupt leaders falling into sexual sin; dishonesty and fraud; disunity and fighting leading to church splits; and all the gossip that goes on about one another. It is tragic, but bad church experiences turn many people away from the faith.

Commitment to the Church Body

What is the application for us? As Christians, we need to stand against the attacks of the evil one on the church. We need to have a higher view of the church and recognize its role in God's kingdom plan. The church is not just a place we come on weekends to see friends or to sing songs. It is not just a place to get our weekly dose of God and be inspired with touching stories. We need to see the high calling God has for the church, that in God's wisdom, the church would be the vehicle to carry to completion what Christ started. It is the means of expanding God's kingdom against the forces of evil and proclaiming His glory.

This means that, practically, we need a deeper commitment to the local church. In reading through the letters of the New Testament, one recurring theme is a call for the church to persevere in unity (see: Ephesians 4:3-6, Philippians 1:27-30, Philippians 4:2-3, Hebrews 10:19-25). Perhaps there was a realization by the leaders that the return of Christ wasn't as soon as they had expected, and they were starting to see people being led astray by trials, persecutions, and false teachings. And so the encouragement was to hold on to the faith and keep the unity of the body in order to stand firm together against Satan's schemes.

There was such an emphasis on working out disagreements, forgiving one another, and not showing favoritism because the authors knew that one way to protect the church from the attacks of Satan was to draw strength and support from one another. If they didn't get along, or had disagreements, then too bad, work it out. The next church was probably many days' travel away.

Nowadays churches are like Starbucks, one on every street corner (sometimes more than one), and the general attitude has become, "Hey, there're so many, find one that's right for you. And if it doesn't fit, look around some more." It's the same kind of mindset the world has for finding a spouse: Date around and see what's best for you, who suits you the most. And if conflicts come up, hey, break up and find someone else who fits better. The commitment (or lack thereof) to our churches and our spouses sadly reflects the radical individualism and gross consumerism of America.

Now, obviously, if your local church is a Korean-speaking church and you don't speak Korean, then that's not a good fit. Or if there are some serious doctrinal errors, then get out of there. But if you are unhappy at church because there are people you don't get along with, don't be surprised to find similar people in every church you go to (any church that has people in it, anyway). Every ministry is going to have weaknesses. But don't forget, the grass is greener where you water it. And sometimes it does take putting on the gloves, getting in the dirt, and working out the issues.

There is value in having different churches with their own culture and there is some truth to the statement "Find a church that is more suitable for you and your gifts." But we have to ask, "For what reason?" Here in America we get so caught up with this idea of choice and everything is marketed so that you can find the best product possible for me and my needs that we carry this attitude over to how we think about church.

But the truth is that church is not about you or me and how our needs can be met. Not primarily, anyway. It is about using our gifts to ultimately bring God the most glory in our community. And the big irony is that it's not until we actually stop thinking about ourselves and start giving ourselves to the church that we are ultimately filled more and more with God. And that's when our needs start being met.

The Lone Medical Ranger

What's with all this church talk? What does all this have to do with applying to medical school? For one, the medical field typically attracts and develops a certain personality and work ethic. Doctors usually get where they are through hard work, self-discipline and perseverance. Sure, they receive help and support along the way, but medicine tends to breed people who are individualistic and self-sufficient, capable of extraordinary accomplishment.

Unfortunately, this attitude carries over to the spiritual life as well. If I have what it takes to be successful in medicine, then surely I can manage my relationship with God on my own if I work hard enough at it. It might not even be a conscious decision, but the self-sufficiency can be so ingrained that it's just how you do things.

> The commitment (or lack thereof) to our churches and our spouses sadly reflects the radical individualism and gross consumerism of America.

Combine a "I can do it myself, there's nothing wrong" attitude and a sub-biblical view of the church, and church is usually one of the first things that goes when classes kick into high gear and you have huge tests coming up week after week. This applies whether you are in high school or medical school and beyond. We are tempted to think, *I have my Bible so I can just fellowship alone with God. Maybe I'll even listen to a sermon while I run on the treadmill. It's the same thing as going to church.* But it is not the same. Friends, we have to be very careful. God did not design us to go through life, and especially difficulties, in isolation.

There are so many practical benefits of being involved in church (if avoiding apostasy isn't enough of a motivation). The church body can help you discover your spiritual gifts and calling. Proverbs 15:22 says, "Plans fail for lack of counsel, but with many advisers they succeed." Other believers who love the Lord can help us pray through God's direction for our life. The church can also provide the accountability we need to be faithful to what we already know is God's will, to spur one another on toward godliness.

But we need to take care because it's not just a matter of missing blessings if I don't come to church, or I will be lonely if all I do is study. Paul makes it very clear that our spiritual vitality is dependent on one another and, depending on where you stand in the Calvin versus Arminius debate, your salvation could be on the line. Many people take "breaks" from church thinking they'll get back into it when things get calmer, but they never end up coming back. They might not flat out renounce Christianity, but they live functionally as non-believers pursuing the same earthly things. I will say again that life doesn't get easier and less busy just because you get a certain degree or job. There will always be temptations to choose from instead of choosing God and the things of God.

* * *

We need the body of Christ on this journey. Apart from the church family, make an effort to meet with other like-minded believers in whatever field you are pursuing. It's easy in training to get caught up with just studying and worrying about passing your classes when you are only around people who stress out about those things all the time. For me, being a part of the school's Christian medical fellowship was so important in helping me maintain the right perspective on life and medicine. And it was through this community that I met Dr. Nick. We need fellow Christians with whom to run the race, and those who have gone before to follow after.

Get involved in your church. Make fellowship with believers a priority in your life. And not just the hang-out-and-having-fun fellowship, but the genuine accountability type of fellowship where people can speak truth into your life. That kind of fellowship requires intentionality. If you are in a season of medical school or residency where things are too busy, it's completely okay to step back from serving. But don't stop going to church altogether. Find a church with multiple services so you can attend post-call or on Saturday. Let your church know when things are hard so they can pray for you and occasionally check up on you. We need to learn to receive love from others (humility!).

If you have set Christ as Lord over your life and have decided to follow wherever He leads you, be on guard because Satan will want to derail your course. We need all the support and prayer we can get. We don't want to just *survive* medical school and residency, or whatever training process you are in. We want to *thrive* physically, emotionally, and spiritually so that when it is all said and done, we have hearts to love as Christ loves, the conviction to carry out God's will instead of our own, and a steadfast faithfulness to Jesus to the very end.

Reflection Questions

1. What are the important relationships in your life? What are you doing to cultivate those relationships?

2. How have you experienced God in community more than you could experience on your own? Are there people in church who have freedom to speak into your life?

3. What is your general attitude toward the institution of the church? Does your current involvement reflect God's high calling for the church?

Part III

Let Me Apply Already!

By the grace God has given me, I laid a foundation as an expert builder, and someone else is building on it. But each one should be careful how he builds. For no one can lay any foundation other than the one already laid, which is Jesus Christ. If any man builds on this foundation using gold, silver, costly stones, wood, hay or straw, his work will be shown for what it is, because the Day will bring it to light. It will be revealed with fire, and the fire will test the quality of each man's work. If what he has built survives, he will receive his reward. If it is burned up, he will suffer loss; he himself will be saved, but only as one escaping through the flames (1 Corinthians 3:10-15).

Chapter 9

A Word About Parents (and to Parents)

ACONVERSATION THAT IS DIFFICULT TO HAVE IS when someone comes for advice because they feel a certain conviction from God, but the parental units disapprove. It's particularly frustrating when the parents profess to be believers as well and are also seeking to follow God's leading. In the context of God's calling and career choices, a large barrier to the advancement of God's kingdom is Christian parents who haven't worked out for themselves what it means for Christ to be Lord of their own lives.

At my church I not only get to work with the youth, but I also have the chance to preach to the parents during their Sunday service. I have had the privilege of building relationships with several of the parents over the years and it is always quite the tight-rope act to maneuver the concerns of both parties, especially regarding their children's futures. Of course, both parties want the best. The tricky part, though, is to get them to see what God's best is. Let's take a look in Scripture to see what insights we can glean:

> Children, obey your parents in the Lord, for this is right. "Honor your father and mother"—which is the first commandment with a promise—"that it may go well with you and that you may enjoy long life on the earth."
>
> Fathers, do not exasperate your children; instead, bring them up in the training and instruction of the Lord (Ephesians 6:1-4).

To the Kids

I wish Paul had provided a little more detail. What does honoring our parents look like? Does that mean we obey every single command? Why does obeying my parents give me long life? What if my parents are wrong? What if they aren't Christians? When can we start making our own decisions? So many questions!

Just to set the context, Paul has been addressing how to live wisely as a Spirit-filled Christian in our relationships with one another. He has described a variety of relationships in the home. The previous section highlighted how husband and wives should interact in Christ. The passage following the one just quoted is about how slaves and masters should treat one other.

Paul's emphasis in these sections is that for everyone in a household, knowing Christ and pleasing God should be the motivation in fulfilling their different roles. Elsewhere the Scriptures remind us that our daily living with one another in Christ is an important witness to the Gospel (see: 1 Peter 3:1-2, Titus 2:1-10).

When he addresses the child-parent relationship, Paul is speaking within the framework of authority that God has set up in the household. The parents are to lead in the home, and the children are to obey.

The obligation of children before God is to obey their parents because God has given parents the duty to set the boundaries for their children by raising them up in the instruction of the Lord. Parents might say you should do this or shouldn't do that "because I said so." But Paul here changes the motivation of obedience to obeying *in the Lord*, in other words, out of respect for Christ Himself. And Paul adds "for this is right." Children obeying parents is pleasing to God. Obeying parents brings them honor, which was huge in the honor-shame culture in which the Ephesians were living.[27]

How does honoring your parents lead to prosperity and long life? There is a "sow and reap" principle built by

God into the natural laws that govern this world. God's design was that good results came about typically if one sowed wisely.[28] If you work hard and diligently, you probably will make a good living. If you treat others well, you probably will have good relationships. If you drink alcohol all day long, your liver will probably eventually fail. Since the parents were responsible for teaching their children how to live, children generally would enjoy long life if they followed their instructions.

Does that mean that the parent's decision is always best, always fair, or always Christian? No, and unfortunately God doesn't make such conditions for this command. The text doesn't say "Children, obey your parents in the Lord, only if what they want is best (or fair, or Christian)." In fact, a parallel passage says "Children, obey your parents in everything, for this pleases the Lord" (Colossians 3:20).

However, the text we're considering does say that children are to obey "in the Lord." If parents command something clearly contrary to God's commands, a discussion needs to happen. How you handle these situations will obviously depend on the specific circumstances, so I won't make any generalized comments on how one should proceed except to say we need a lot of prayer and counsel, particularly from our pastors and other godly mentors.

But if we are honest, it is not so common that parents desire something clearly contrary to Scripture, like forcing you to worship idols or denounce God. I think children disobey parents more often than parents command something against Scripture. I am in no way minimizing or disregarding the very real persecution that can happen within the family when a child converts to Christianity from a different faith upbringing. But in our American Christianity, children disobey usually because they think their parents are being unreasonable, or because of their own sinful tendencies.

Does this mean we can't disagree with our parents? No, of course not. Honoring our parents involves engaging them in discussion to hear their viewpoint and to share ours. If you are fortunate enough to have Christian parents, it is an invitation to enter into prayer with them. But it does mean that if after prayer and discussion your parents still stand on their decision and that decision is not in direct contradiction to God's Word, God commands us as children to submit to their authority. Remember that your parents will ultimately be held accountable before God in the exercise of their authority, so continue to pray for your parents if you feel they are not hearing God correctly.

> A large barrier to the advancement of God's kingdom is Christian parents who haven't worked out for themselves what it means for Christ to be Lord of their own lives.

When does this command for children to obey their parents expire? While talking about marriage Paul quotes Genesis in Ephesians 5:31: "For this reason a man will leave his father and mother and be united to his wife, and the two will become one flesh." When we are no longer under our parent's household, we are free to pursue what we think is God's will. Our parents will have to realize that one day we have to assume responsibility for our own lives and our own families.

But the command to honor our parents is life-long. While in our parents' household, we honor them by obeying them in the Lord. When we move out, we can still honor our parents by seeking their wisdom and counsel, but we are no longer obligated to obey if they disagree. When parents get older, we honor them by looking after them and caring for their physical needs.[29]

Some of us, particularly those of us who are Asian living also in a shame-based culture, need to remember that we answer ultimately to God and not to our parents. Our problem is typically not one of rebellion, but one of obedience. We are so afraid of not pleasing them and getting their disapproval that we dare not pursue anything that could potentially displease them. While under their authority we are hesitant to engage them in discussion of our faith, and even when we are free to make our own decisions, their voice sometimes is louder than God's. Our parents can become idols like anything else. Recall that Jesus said obeying Him could mean persecution, even from within your own family (Matthew 10:21-22). Jesus also redefined the concept of family beyond bloodlines to include those involved in carrying out God's will (Mark 3:31-35).

This is a topic that is too large and complex to unpack in just a few pages. The water is getting muddier as children are remaining dependent on their parents for longer periods while they pursue higher education (or simply to play, prolonging young adulthood) and delaying marriage. My intention isn't to solve any problems, but just to stir up some thoughtful prayer on how we can honor our parents by pursuing Jesus. And prayer is the operative word here.

On my own journey, I have been more fortunate than most. Even though my parents are not believers, and though they disapprove of the path I have chosen, they have trusted me to make the right decisions for my own life. That trust didn't come automatically, though. It was gradually given after seeing what God had done in my life through my willingness to follow after Him over the years, and how I have tried to obey and honor them along the way.

But like in many Asian families, my relationship with my parents has been mostly performance-based. Because we never developed a healthier means of communication, I learned to relate to my parents through my accomplishments. It didn't help that my Mandarin is terrible. (Yes, I was born in Taiwan. It's shameful that I can barely speak my native tongue.)

Something you can do is start working on your communication with your parents. The more you are able to talk to them about everyday life things, the easier it will be to talk about big life-altering decisions. We have a tendency to hide what we think or just give up because there's a language barrier. But again, part of honoring our parents is including them in the thoughts behind our decision making.

A huge breakthrough in my relationship with my own parents was when I mustered the courage to say "I love you" sometime during my college years. I'm pretty sure my parents told me they loved me when I was little, but I can't remember them ever saying it to me later while I was growing up. It wasn't until college when I decided to tell my mom that I loved her. It took a little longer to say it to my dad. Just the idea of doing that is absolutely terrifying to some, who would rather show their love by getting straight A's! It wasn't a magical thing, but it did break down some walls and empowered me to be more open with them, especially when they started saying it back.

When I decided to go into seminary, I ended up writing a letter to them sharing about my faith and how God had brought me to this place. It wasn't the best way to communicate, but at the very least they were able to hear my reasoning behind it and realize it wasn't just a spur-of-the-moment decision. They expressed their concerns, and I suspect they will continue to voice their thoughts. I pray God will give me words that are gracious and a resolve to obey Him, trusting that my life decisions can bear witness to the gospel in their lives.

All this talk about parents reminds me that I haven't called them in awhile. I miss them.

To the Parents (and Future Parents)

I qualify everything that follows in this section by saying I have no idea what it is like to be a parent. I have no idea what it is like to give up my life to raise a child. I have no idea what it is like when that child goes down a path I think is unwise or even blatantly dangerous. I only know what the Scriptures say and what my experiences with my parents and the parents of the youth at church have taught me. I hope when I'm a parent I will still hold fast to these principles.

Now that Priscilla and I have been married for two years, the big question has been, "When are you going to have kids?" Especially my parents, every time they visit they'll ask about it in some way. I've always wanted to be a dad. I loved kids and babies while I was growing up so I thought I would just start a family right away. But now that we are married we are seeing more and more what a huge responsibility parenting is. It's not an encouraging sign when couples who have kids keep urging us to wait and enjoy our time together. We are realizing that a lot of the issues we are dealing with today are related to how we were raised by our parents. I still want to be dad, but I think my eagerness has been tempered a little bit with some reality. Much kudos to those of you who are parents; it is a high calling.

Again, I wish Paul was as verbose on this topic as he was on the gospel message. He simply says, "Fathers, do not exasperate your children; instead, bring them up in the training and instruction of the Lord." The New American Standard Bible reads, "Fathers, do not provoke your children to anger, but bring them up in the discipline and instruction of the Lord."

In other words, fathers don't treat your children in a way that will make them angry or bitter. God has given the father authority in the household, but that authority needs to be exercised with care and sensitivity. In the category of "provoking your children to anger" is taking out your anger or frustrations on your children, overly harsh words, insults, and unreasonable demands and expectations. For sure, mothers play a hugely significant role in the raising of children, but Paul's charge is directed solely to fathers as heads of their households.[30]

Working in the youth group made up of primarily Asian Americans, I have to say that "exasperated" is a good word to describe what some of the youth are feeling. They go from school to tutoring to weekend SAT classes, and some are starting these in junior high (and don't forget the tennis and music lessons, school club involvement, and hospital volunteering). There is such pressure to get a certain GPA and SAT score in order to get into prestigious schools and a particular career path or else their entire futures are ruined. I am for sure a fan of hard work and good grades, but we can't just care only about their academic well-being.

> There is no question that you love your children. But the question is do you love Jesus more than your children?

The pattern from Scripture is that the parents, and particularly fathers, have the ultimate responsibility of raising their children in the "training and instruction of the Lord." This includes training them in the understanding of the Christian faith and how to live it out. It involves familiarizing them with Bible, God's kingdom purposes, and the mission, teaching, and example of Christ. But in our Western world today, we seem to have things backwards. It seems like the father's main role is to make money while the mother does the majority of the child-rearing. Schools and the media give children their education and identity, and church does the spiritual formation.

There is a movement questioning if youth ministry is even biblical because parents are the ones who are to be raising their children in the Lord.[31] For some, spiritual training has been relegated to the youth pastor, while in the homes very little discussion happens about God or matters of faith. I was saved through youth ministry so I definitely appreciate its value, but there is truth to some of these criticisms of youth ministry. As we have served in the youth group, we are realizing we can't do this on our own. We get kids for a couple of hours a week to try to give them biblical teaching, but that is just not enough compared to the worldly messages they are inundated with the rest of the week. And unfortunately, some of those worldly messages come from the Christian home.

I want to make clear I understand that, as parents, you want the absolute best for your children. Many of you are very good at not living for your own pleasure and comfort. Some of you have spent your life living for others, and in particular, for your children. You didn't buy that nice car or expensive dress, or go on that dream vacation so your child could have a nicer car to drive, enjoy the prom, or go to that Ivy League school. Some of you have worked hard day after day, year after year (for some, multiple jobs), in order to provide all the opportunities and even more for your children.

There is no question that you love your children. But the question is do you love Jesus more than your children?

Put another way, are your children's relationships with Jesus more important to you than their worldly successes? Is it most important to you that your child not just know facts about Jesus, but has a willingness to share in Christ's sufferings by obeying God's will in his or her life? Understand that how you raise your children has tremendous impact on how their relationship with God develops. What you value will be very much a part of their value system and what they seek after.

We have been talking about how important it is for one to find his or her identity in Christ, as a child of God, instead of trying to find it in what their hands can accomplish. One way we learn that is through the model of our own parents. If you look through the Bible, people drew their identities from their fathers. David wasn't just David, he was David, son of Jesse. Isaiah wasn't just Isaiah, he was Isaiah, son of Amoz. Jesus wasn't just Jesus, He was Jesus, the Son of God. Their identities were very much wrapped up in who their fathers were.

We have lost much of that in our individualistic culture today. With an increasing number of broken families and single mothers, we have a generation of children growing up without any idea of who their fathers are. And our relationship with our earthly fathers drastically colors the way we view God, our heavenly Father. If I am only significant to my earthly father when I get perfect grades, or accomplish this or that, or pursue a certain profession, then God must not accept me unless I am a better person, or I do this or that, or I am a doctor, engineer, or whatever else.

Parents, you need to teach your children that their worth is not dependent on what they can do. You need to remind them often that your love for them is based on who they are: your child. That doesn't mean you don't discipline them. It doesn't mean you don't encourage them to do well in school. That doesn't mean you let them go to all the church activities and allow them do whatever they want. You still have to do responsible parenting.

But it does mean you need to be intentional in caring for your children's souls. My friend shared with me that in high school, all he heard his dad say to him during the week was, "Did you do your homework?" and "Did you practice your violin?" Granted, that parent was not a Christian, but Christian parents, how often do you ask about your children's quiet time and what God has been teaching them? When was the last time you considered their spiritual gifting and what God may be calling them to? When was the last time you prayed with your children or asked for prayer requests?

These conversations will be tremendously awkward if you are not used to having them with your children. Do not be surprised if your child doesn't want to engage with you. They are probably thinking, *Why are we talking about this all of a sudden now?* Please don't give up. It takes time for new, healthier lines of communication and ways of relating to develop.

And when your children come to you with their hearts, take the time to nurture them. They may come to you one day with dreams to pursue a certain career. Don't shut them down right away because that job won't be able to pay the bills or attract a spouse. Explore with them why they want to pursue that particular vocation. It may be a passing fad. Or there might be a talent just waiting to be revealed. Remember, you job as a parent is not to choose God's will for them. Not every child is called to be a doctor, engineer, or a lawyer. Your job as a parent is to raise your children up in Christ and help them to discern God's will for their life and to discover their unique giftings and calling.

The message in the home must be different from the message your children are getting from the world, which is: You are only something if you have money, or a prestigious job, or a lot of things. No, we need to communicate to our children that we are proud of them and love them regardless of what they can do. Of course, celebrate with them when they are successful, but also encourage them when they aren't, letting them know you are still on their side. If you don't, you will be setting your children up for failure, because, ultimately, nothing we can do or accomplish will allow us to attain the significance we are designed for as God's children.

It is worth pointing out that just because both parents are physically in a home doesn't mean all is well either. There are many functionally (not functional) single parent families with one parent, typically the father, distant or absent because all of the energy and time is spent pursuing a career, most likely with great intentions to provide opportunities he never enjoyed for his family. But there is also a cost. Yes, we should be working hard at our jobs and watching out for our family's financial well-being. We should be good stewards of what God has entrusted to us.

There is no sin in providing for our children and making sure they are taken care of when we are gone. That's a worthwhile legacy to leave behind.

But will you also leave behind a spiritual legacy based upon how you lived and what you did with God's gifts. If so, your children will know the blessings of what it is like to follow after God and put Him first. Will you invest in your children with the same zeal and energy, raising them up in the instruction of the Lord? Because, more important to you will not be whether or not your kids can be put through an Ivy League school, or if they will have houses to inherit after you die, or even if they become world-renowned physicians. Far more important to you will be if you see them again in heaven, standing unashamed before God because they embraced Christ, held on to the faith, and are covered by His blood.

> Your job as a parent is to raise your children up in Christ and help them to discern God's will for their life and to discover their unique giftings and calling.

*   *   *

Our relationship with our parents can be a tremendous source of stress and frustration. But it can also be a wellspring of support and encouragement. Parents, you are also included in the call to make disciples of all nations, and that starts in the home. What an influence you can have if you teach your child to love God first and foremost. Children, what a testimony it can be to the world if you are able to seek God's will together with your parents.

To my own parents, thank you for all your love and support. I'm sorry for the ways that I have hurt you and the headaches I have caused, whether intentionally or unintentionally. I thank God He has given you to me as my parents. I hope that, in my life choices, you have been able to see tangibly the God in whom I have put my trust. It is my earnest prayer that you will both come to know Jesus Christ as your personal savior as well. I love you.

Reflection Questions

1. How much of your current pursuits are influenced by your parents' desires?

2. Has your desire to obey God ever come into conflict with obedience to your parents? How did you handle those situations? In what ways can your communication with them improve?

3. If you are a parent, has it been hard to trust God to lead your child?

Chapter 10

Don't Worry,
Be Saved

YOU HAVE MADE CHRIST YOUR LORD. YOU HAVE counted the cost. You have prayed and sought counsel, and it seems pretty clear that medicine is the way to go. You really don't want the false promises of this world. Yet the doubts still remain:

How am I going to pay off my massive school debt?

If I become a missionary or work in the inner city, how will I be able to support my future family?

How will I be taken care of in the future if I don't save up now?

What if I do this and I fail miserably?

If these thoughts and worries have never crossed your mind, then perhaps you've never really risked much for the Lord. If you have never been anxious, then likely you have given out of your excess, what you can afford to sacrifice. Or you are super godly with tremendous faith. If that's the case, I want to read your book.

Insecurity is a consequence of our separation from God, from whom we derive all security as His children. Even after we have made our relationship right with God, our tendency to worry still plagues us. Some experience anxiety stronger than others, but it will be with us until we are complete in Christ. How can we be freed from these earthly worries that prevent us from following God's will for our lives? We need to detach from the things of this world and attach to Christ, seeking God's kingdom instead of our own. Consider the words of Jesus:

> *Then Jesus said to his disciples: "Therefore I tell you, do not worry about your life, what you will eat; or about your body, what you will wear. Life is more than food, and the body more than clothes. Consider the ravens: They do not sow or reap, they have no storeroom or barn; yet God feeds them. And how much more valuable you are than birds! Who of you by worrying can add a single hour to his life? Since you cannot do this very little thing, why do you worry about the rest?*

Consider how the lilies grow. They do not labor or spin. Yet I tell you, not even Solomon in all his splendor was dressed like one of these. If that is how God clothes the grass of the field, which is here today, and tomorrow is thrown into the fire, how much more will he clothe you, O you of little faith! And do not set your heart on what you will eat or drink; do not worry about it. For the pagan world runs after all such things, and your Father knows that you need them. But seek his kingdom, and these things will be given to you as well.

Do not be afraid, little flock, for your Father has been pleased to give you the kingdom. Sell your possessions and give to the poor. For where your treasure is, there your heart will be also" (Luke 12:22-34).

If you recall, this passage comes right after the parable about the rich man storing up wealth for himself so he could enjoy the rest of his life. Jesus' point in that story was that we need to be rich toward God and not toward ourselves. As Jesus talked, the disciples perhaps thought to themselves, *Great story Jesus, but if I give up everything for you, who's going to take care of me in the future?*

And so, Jesus proceeded to paint a picture of God the Father's complete provision. Notice that He was addressing just His disciples. What follows applies to those who have given up everything to follow after Jesus. It is not a blanket promise.

Jesus started by pointing out that life is more than simply trying to get food and clothing. This life isn't just about providing for our physical bodies; we were created for much more than that. He then made a couple of observations about God's created order to teach that God will take care of His creation.

Birds don't have any fancy retirement plan, Jesus reminded them, yet God feeds them. And not just any birds. God takes care of even the ravens, those "unclean" birds (Leviticus 11:15). What about the grass of the field? They don't have any capability to work, yet they are dressed better than the richest of kings. God is their Creator and He takes care of them.

What is Jesus getting at? If God takes care of His creation by providing food and clothing, how will He not provide for the pinnacle of His creation? Remember, after God created man it was very good. We are His beloved for whom He didn't even spare His only Son. God knows our needs. He knows everyone's worries. Jesus' encouragement is to seek

> If you have never been anxious, then likely you have given out of your excess, what you can afford to sacrifice.

God and His kingdom first. Not only will you inherit an everlasting kingdom in the next life, but you will also be provided for in this one.[32]

So the solution to the problem of excess worry about how this life will turn out is, first of all, to remind ourselves of our identity: God's children. God will meet the physical needs of His children. Again, this is not a promise for everyone. Jesus was talking to His disciples, those committed to follow after Christ. Yes, God is the father of all people in the sense that He is the Creator of mankind. But the Bible is clear that the identity of a child of God is reserved for those who have placed their faith in Jesus Christ. John 1:12 says, "Yet to all who received him, to those who believed in his name, he gave the right to become children of God." With our new identity comes the promise of not just the inheritance of God's kingdom in the future, but also God's provision for His children in this life. We do have to keep in mind that our idea of provision may be different, and that God is not in the business of making us comfortable.

So how do we stop worrying? We certainly can't just will it to be so. We need to let the Holy Spirit redeem the lie that we can achieve security in what our hands can accomplish, whether that is getting into a good school, securing a great job, or racking up big savings. If you are not a Christian, understand that no amount of accomplishments or money will bring you the security you are searching for. Ironically, the more money you make, the more you worry about losing it. The security we are looking for is only found in God, and the only way to have a restored relationship with God is through faith in His Son Jesus for the forgiveness of sins.

For those of us who are Christians, we need to meditate deeply and often on the truth that our security, and really, our everything, is found in our identity as God's children. We are loved and accepted completely in Christ by God.

We need to declare along with Paul in Philippians 3:8, "What is more, I consider everything a loss compared to the surpassing greatness of knowing Christ Jesus my Lord, for whose sake I have lost all things."

We need an attachment to Jesus Christ, but in order to attach our heart completely to Him, we need to first detach it from the things of this world. Unfortunately, this world does such a great job in calling out to us, doesn't it? Thanksgiving just passed as I wrote this. During Black Friday weekend and Cyber Monday week, I must confess I was glued to the Internet looking for the next great deal. Even stuff I didn't want, just by looking at the pictures, reading the reviews, and seeing the discount, in my heart I felt the "Ooo, I want that." My heart just started attaching to all these different things. It's good to be reminded of Paul's warnings to Timothy:

> *But godliness with contentment is great gain. For we brought nothing into the world, and we can take nothing out of it. But if we have food and clothing, we will be content with that. People who want to get rich fall into temptation and a trap and into many foolish and harmful desires that plunge men into ruin and destruction. For the love of money is a root of all kinds of evil. Some people, eager for money, have wandered from the faith and pierced themselves with many griefs (1 Timothy 6:6-10).*

Godliness with contentment is great gain. We brought nothing in, we can take nothing out. If we have food and clothing, we will be content with that. How can Paul think this way? Because he knows his relationship with God is secure and that God is his provider. He says in Philippians 4:12-13, "I have learned the secret of being content in any and every situation, whether well fed or hungry, whether living in plenty or in want. I can do everything through him who gives me strength." Wow, what a perspective. Notice that trusting in God in every circumstance is something he learned. It is not automatic and certainly is not obvious. Imagine what your life would look like with that mindset. Imagine the kind of freedom you would have to serve God with your all.

How do we detach from the desires for all this worthless stuff that is here today and gone tomorrow? It's got to be through prayer and meditation on passages like these that remind us of what has eternal value, and what will just be burned up by the flames. We also need to be reminded of how beautiful Jesus is and what is in store for us in heaven. Just as our hearts attach to earthly things the more we look at them, read reviews about them, try them out, and think about having them, we attach to Christ the more we read about, think about, talk about, and experience Christ as we live in obedience to God's Word.

God calls us not just to detach from our love for material things, but also to detach from our selfish ambitions and dreams. Jesus' solution to worry is not only to remember that God provides for His children. Jesus also encourages us to seek first the kingdom of God.

If it is God's kingdom we are trying to build up and God who gives us the abilities, then really, we can leave the results up to Him. It's His kingdom after all, right? I'm sure He cares about its success much more than we do. We are freed from having to perform and meet certain expectations that we, our parents, and the world have placed on us. We can simply give our best and trust the rest to God.

The Birds

My first quarter of college was a big adjustment. I didn't like the fact that in college your grade was based mostly on a couple of tests. Gone were the homework and extra credit points that padded my grades in high school. I remember being in a Medieval English Literature class having to read books that, to put it technically, were weird. The first book I had to read was about a knight storming a castle in order to rescue a rose. Supposedly it was an allegory of some sort of sexual encounter. I didn't get it. Not surprisingly, I got a C on my first paper.

I wasn't used to getting C's so I began to worry big time. I started thinking to myself: *I'm going to get a C in this class and then I won't be able to get into medical school and therefore my parents will disown me and I'll never be able to find a decent job, so I will never meet anybody who will marry me, and inevitably I will spend the rest of my life lonely, working a job I hate, and dying poor and forgotten.*

A little dramatic, I agree, but if we are honest, it's not too far off the mark of what goes on in our minds, no? And I was a Christian. At that time I was pretty good with

Scripture memorization and I had memorized the Matthew version of Jesus' teaching on not worrying. One day I was sitting in that class, not even paying attention to the professor because I was worrying about all these things, staring up into the high vaulted ceilings. All of a sudden, a bird flew through an open window and started flying around in the classroom.

At that moment, God brought this passage alive in my heart and I was convinced that God would take care of me, whatever it was that I did, as long as I sought after God's kingdom. From that day on I had such a confidence and peace when it came to grades and tests. And I have taken a lot of tests, let me tell you. I was still pretty prideful and I went on to struggle with doing things in my own strength, but this was not merely a trust in my own abilities. God opened my eyes to the truth that He is trustworthy.

> In order to attach our heart completely to Christ, we need to first detach it from the things of this world.

Some who know me might think: *No Jack, this is a stupid illustration. You are just smart so you would have gotten an A anyway.* I don't know, maybe. But honestly, in high school I wasn't a superstar student. I did pretty well, but not straight A's, 1600 SAT status (or 2400 or whatever it is now)—not even close. But college and on was such a different story. You have to take my word for it that God did a supernatural work in my heart, like the peace that surpasses understanding that Paul speaks of in Philippians 4:6-7.

I know that applying Jesus' words about God providing for birds and grass to my anxiety about Medieval Literature wasn't exactly good "hermeneutics" since the passage is really talking about God's provision for our physical needs.[33] But more broadly, the point is to trust God to provide for all our needs, instead of trying to secure (and in some cases, maximize) everything in our own strength.

Believing is Seeing

Before I applied to Talbot for seminary, Priscilla and I thought much about how we would be able to manage everything financially. I never understood why seminary education was so expensive given the amount of money most pastors and church workers make after graduation. School was going to be a huge investment, both in time and money, so I wanted confirmation that this was the right path to take.

Not too long into this decision process, I received in the mail a flyer from the local car dealership requesting to buy my car. To draw potential customers, each flyer had a winning code to redeem a prize simply for showing up. The rewards ranged from gift cards to flat-screen TVs to the grand prize, twenty-five thousand dollars. I really thought to myself, *God, this is it! If I get this prize money, then for sure seminary is where you want me to be.*

And so I drove down to the dealership and presented my winning code. The salesperson came back with a box full of envelopes for me to choose from, wishing me luck. I picked one at random, and with a slight tremble in my hands and an ever so light flutter of my heart, I opened the envelope and found . . . a five dollar gift card. At first I felt some disappointment. But then I realized I had five more dollars than I'd had thirty seconds earlier, and not getting the twenty-five thousand dollars in no way nullified God's trustworthiness.

As Christians, God calls us to walk by faith, not by sight. Often, though, we want to see first before we believe that God is leading us the right way. First Kings 17 tells the story of a poor widow and her son during a time of severe drought. They were on the verge of starvation, and the woman was out gathering sticks to prepare their very last meal. There she encountered a man of God, the prophet Elijah, who asked her for water and food. The following dialogue is found in 1 Kings 17:12-14:

> "As surely as the Lord your God lives," she replied, "I don't have any bread—only a handful of flour in a jar and a little oil in a jug. I am gathering a few sticks to take home and make a meal for myself and my son, that we may eat it—and die."

> Elijah said to her, "Don't be afraid. Go home and do as you have said. But first make a small cake of bread for me from what you have and bring it to me, and then make something for yourself and your son. For this is what the Lord, the God of Israel, says: 'The jar of flour will not be used up and

*the jug of oil will not run dry until the day the
Lord gives rain on the land.'"*

Imagine you are this widow, and you are one meal
away from watching your child die from starvation. A
stranger hits you up for some food, asking you to make
him something first out of the very little you have left, and
promising some magical unlimited flour and oil in return.
I would probably be thinking, *You must be crazy. Why
don't I make some bread for me and my son first and see
if the flour and oil will keep on coming?*

We like our ducks lined up before "stepping out in
faith." Funny thing is that God has already laid it out for
us. If you haven't read the Bible yet, here's the spoiler:
Christ will return in glory and God's kingdom will be ush-
ered in full. On that day, we will realize that the things we
gave up in faith for God's kingdom really weren't much at
all compared to all that God has in store for His children.
Sometimes God only shows us enough to take the next
step. But look far down the path and take heart that God
has taken care of the end.

The widow stepped out in faith and did exactly as Elijah requested. The result? "So there was food every day
for Elijah and for the woman and her family. For the jar
of flour was not used up and the jug of oil did not run dry,
in keeping with the word of the Lord spoken by Elijah"
(1 Kings 17:15-16).

Looking back, it's been amazing to see God provide for
us in this decision to put His kingdom first. I already mentioned the school nurse job my wife got even though she was

not the most qualified. My church has also been able to provide a partial scholarship for tuition.

The doors God opens, no one can close. If God has called you to a particular task, He will take care of the details. That of course doesn't mean we just sit around and do nothing. We still have the choice of whether or not to go through those doors. We have to be sensitive to the Spirit's leading and discern which doors are of God and which are of our own selfish desires. God may give us signs of confirmation, but the ultimate confirmation is in His unrelenting faithfulness to His people as evidenced throughout the Scriptures, and in the life, death, and resurrection of His Son, Jesus Christ.

It's good to keep in mind that Jesus didn't exactly give His disciples a play-by-play handbook when He sent them out to proclaim the kingdom. No, He told them to just go, don't take anything, and stay with anyone who will house you. When Jesus was about to depart from this earth, entrusting His disciples with the most important mission in all of human history, He basically told them not to worry about it, hang out until the Holy Spirit comes, and then He will teach you what to do and say.

As children of God, we have the promise of 1 John 5:14-15: "This is the confidence we have in approaching God: that if we ask anything according to His will, he hears us. And if we know that he hears us—whatever we ask—we know that we have what we asked of him." We have a God who hears the prayers of His children, and answers them.

Does that mean that we will get straight A's and get everything that we ask for? Clearly not. We don't necessarily need straight A's, the best Ivy League school, or the most efficient path in order to be what God has prepared for us (although that could be God's plan). The key, of course, is praying according to God's will, and not our own. But, most of the time, we have an idea of what would be the best plan for my life. We have our own agenda and timetable of which college we're supposed to go to for this period of time so that by a certain age we will have this degree and that girlfriend on our way to having the ideal life.

If we look through the Bible, we see that God's idea of time is quite different from ours. Abraham was seventy-five years old when God called him to leave his homeland (Genesis 12:4) and Isaac wasn't born until Abraham was one hundred years old (Genesis 21:5). Joseph was seventeen when he first started having his dreams (Genesis 37:2) and thirty years old when he was finally lifted up in Pharaoh's court (Genesis 41:46). About half a millennium would pass after Israel's exile before Jesus would come on the scene. Two thousand years later we are still looking forward for Christ's return.

> We should trust God to provide for all our needs, instead of trying to secure (and in some cases, maximize) everything in our own strength.

If God's chief concern were convenience and comfort, history would look pretty different. It probably would be over by now. Instead, God's chief concern is His glory and whatever process that will maximize that. We live in an age of instant noodles, instant messaging, and instant gratification. We want things and we want them now (if not now, then preferably next day delivery). We get upset when our Internet lags or our friends don't text us back within ten seconds. But sometimes, prayers are not answered immediately. Some do not get answered in our lifetime.

Second Peter 3:8 reminds us that God's idea of time is different: "With the Lord a day is like a thousand years, and a thousand years are like a day." This is a good thing, because there are more people God wants to save. God has been unfolding a beautiful drama of salvation throughout history, and our lives are but a small part of God's story. Yes, there are things that God wants to do in our individual lives now, but somehow all of it fits into God's sovereign plan.

The deeper question is, "Is God trustworthy?" Is God's will really better than ours? If things are not panning out the way I have envisioned, can I trust that somehow if God's will is accomplished, it is better than anything I can come up with? God's provision is going to look different for everyone, and it definitely will look different from what the world considers as provision. For some it might mean success and influence to impact others for the kingdom. For others it might simply be faith and strength to stand up under persecution and suffering. Can we be content with what God has in store for us and pray along with Jesus, "Not my will, but yours be done" (Luke 22:42)?

Trusting Again . . . and Again

I wish that once we decide to trust Jesus for our salvation, we would automatically be able to trust Him with every other decision that we make after that. After all, the most important decision has been made, right? But trusting in Jesus over our anxieties and desires is something we have to do over and over again. It took faith to trust God with choosing family medicine. After residency it was again a leap of faith to enroll in seminary and focus more on ministry.

In God's providence, I stayed on an extra year after residency to do a faculty development fellowship. Even though I had never thought much about academic medicine, I discovered that I really enjoyed teaching. After that fellowship year, I seriously considered the academic route. It would be a nice career, a good balance between patient care, teaching, and doing projects that I'm interested in—not to mention great county benefits. A faculty position even opened up at my residency program, so it looked like the stars were aligning. But God began to put on my heart the ministry at church and a desire to go to seminary. It became clear that to get involved at the level that I wanted and to keep working full-time would really be asking for my personal life and marriage to fall apart. I had to choose.

It was hard not choosing to advance myself professionally since I've been working so hard these past gazillion years getting that medical degree. Even now, the doubts and worries come up here and again. Who knows if the opportunity to get into academics will be there in the future? It would be nice to make a name for myself in the medical field. I'm not asking for much, maybe just a disease named after me or something. The "Tsai virus" has a nice ring to it, don't you think? My dad left some pretty big shoes to fill being a well-known anesthesiologist in Taiwan with a PhD under his belt, tons of papers under his name, and experience as a hospital administrator.

Even as I was doing my edits on this book, my dad sent an e-mail telling me about a book chapter he helped to write on transesophageal echocardiography that had just been published. And here I am trying to write a book on Christian discipleship? I look at all that he has accomplished professionally and a part of me says, "Ooo, I want those earthly accolades." (I actually don't use the word "accolades" when I talk to myself, but you know what I mean.)

And what about my choice to go into ministry? Thinking about my church, who knows what will happen and how long the ministry will be around. What if I drive all the people away? What if I don't do well in seminary? How discouraging would that be? How about writing this book? What was I even thinking? And on and on go the attacks of the evil one, firing worries after worries.

With Satan filling our minds constantly with his lies and egging on our ego and pride, we have to daily remind ourselves of the cross and our identity in Christ as God's children. We need to attach to Christ daily. We also need to detach from the desires of this world and our cravings to find significance and security in our accomplishments, our possessions, and our status.

Let us center our hearts on God's steadfast faithfulness to those who trust in His Son Jesus. Let us be reminded of Romans 8:32 that God "who did not spare his own Son, but gave him up for us all—how will he not also, along with him, graciously give us all things?" I don't know what the future looks like, but I want to be faithful to what He has shown me now. God certainly hasn't let me down yet.

* * *

Despite this encouragement, you may continue to worry about how the whole finances thing will work out. Never mind that even the lowest paying job of the lowest paying medical specialty pays way more than the average salary in the United States. But I will grant you that wanting to serve God overseas or in resource-poor areas can be a difficult choice if you are graduating with a six figure educational debt.

There are options, such as the National Health Service Corps, that provide scholarships to those pursuing primary care in physician-shortage areas.[34] Many community clinics also offer loan repayment programs as part of their compensation package. If you are interested in a career in medical missions, MedSend is just one organization that offers grants to repay your loans while you are away on the field.[35]

So ask yourself again, "Do I really believe that God is trustworthy?" You may not become rich compared to your doctor friends. I'm not making that much more than I did as a resident, but it is enough. It might mean adjusting your standards of living a bit, but God will meet the needs of His children and provide for you treasures that will never be stolen or lost. I pray that in response to God's convictions in your heart, in light of the cross, you can answer, "Yes

God, you are trustworthy. You have made the ultimate provision for my deepest need in your Son, Jesus Christ. Whatever happens to me in this life, if it will bring glory to You, I will embrace it and give You praise. I'm not going to worry that things are not going my way. I'm saved."

Reflection Questions

1. About what do you tend to worry the most? What do you do with those worries?

2. In what ways has God provided for you in the past?

3. If you had nothing but Jesus, would that be enough?

Chapter 11

More Than
Ordinary

ALL OF US WANT LIVES THAT ARE SIGNIFICANT. WE want our lives to have meaning, to accomplish something worthwhile with our time here, Christian or not. I don't think any of us as kids dreamed that one day we would get to work a job we hate just to make enough money to pay the bills and live for the weekends and the two weeks of vacation we get all year.

No, we want more than the ordinary. Unfortunately, attaining that goal is not so simple. Many start off with admirable dreams and good intentions. We may even be in the exact vocation God has for us. But, somewhere along the way, our priorities and goals change, and we get side-tracked into lives that have little eternal impact. We need to take care because this world offers plenty of temporary substitutes people end up settling for.

I'm not sure exactly how this plays out for girls, but for guys, you can really see it in our choices of entertainment. We all love epic action movies because it sweeps us up into a greater adventure, a battle between good and evil. Think also about the millions of dollars spent on professional and collegiate sporting events. There's something about the competition, the team working toward a common goal that speaks to us. It takes us beyond ourselves and the day-to-day grind of life.

It's the same thing with video games. You hear about people who don't shower because they must play games for days on end. And this is not just with high school students who we think should know better. Video game addiction is becoming a huge problem even among adults. There are horrifying stories of people dying from heart attacks and pulmonary embolisms after playing video games for ridiculous amounts of time. There are even instances of children of gaming parents who die from neglect.[36] There has to be something diabolical going on behind some of these things.

How can a person play so much, we wonder? It can't be just because the games are fun, although they may be. There's something deeper, something spiritual, perhaps sinister. It may sound strange, but the leveling up, gaining special powers, and prevailing against enemies speak to a deep-seated need in our soul. It is that need to be significant and powerful, our pride's desire for self-glory. These games let us escape the "ordinariness" of our lives into a world where our actions can actually have great impact.

I don't mean to pick on video games since I've played my fair share. There are even some benefits to gaming; for example, people who play actually seem to do better in certain surgical procedures. But there are ungodly games just as there are ungodly movies, TV shows, and books. I'm not saying we have to be reading our Bibles, praying, and going on mission trips every moment of our free time. God desires us to rest and even provides for our enjoyment (1 Timothy 6:17), but many people live simply from weekend to weekend, being consumed by these trivial pursuits.

The Gospel, Again

We live in a society that craves significance, with people seeking to be noticed by posting videos and pictures of themselves all over the Internet and sending them to reality competition shows. Why is that? Well, part of it is that we were created to play a significant role in God's plan. Mankind was to be God's image bearers and display God's glory, character, and greatness throughout creation. We were also created to live forever, so the idea of living insignificant, forgotten lives is contrary to our nature.

Remember again the story of the tower of Babel. God told the survivors of the flood in Genesis 9 to go and fill the earth. Their job was to image God's glory throughout all of creation. Two chapters later, we find the people settling down and building for themselves a city. Why? Genesis 11:4 is worth repeating because it speaks so poignantly about our deep desires for significance and security: "Come, let us build ourselves a city, with a tower that reaches to the heavens, so that we may make a name for ourselves and not be scattered over the face of the whole earth." They wanted to be like God, and they wanted the security of a city's protective walls.

Every one of us is an eternal being, originally created for eternity with God in perfect intimacy and fellowship. But we know that because Adam and Eve crossed the boundaries God set for them, all of us have subsequently sinned and rebelled against God. Instead of living in perfect fellowship with God, we are now separated from Him and destined for

> We need to take care because this world offers plenty of temporary substitutes people end up settling for.

death. Not just physical death, but the spiritual death of eternal separation from God in hell.

The Bible tells us that there is no way to mend our relationship with God except through Jesus Christ, who lived a perfect life and died on the cross to take on the punishment for our sins. And through confessing our sins and trusting in Jesus as our Lord and savior we can have a restored relationship with God. But instead, men have rejected God and turned to themselves to try to make sense of this life. We have eternity set in our hearts as

Ecclesiastes 3:11 says, yet we are so very aware of our own mortality. As a result, men and women throughout history have spent their lives in vain trying to make a name for themselves here in this life apart from God.

While God has given us many good things for us to enjoy as we live for Him, whether it be sports, movies, or games, we have the temptation of turning to those gifts to fulfill that which only the Giver can fulfill. It can even happen to the dreams and aspirations God has placed in our hearts. Instead of using whatever vocation God has called them to for His ultimate glory, many have poured out their lives advancing in their fields for their own glory, comfort, and pleasure. The truth is that all of us, Christians or not, are worshippers. We all give our hearts to something. If not God, then it will be something else: money, sex, job, family, hobbies, dreams, and even church service. These are what the Bible calls idols. And we know how God feels about idols.

So it all has to start with reconciling our relationship with God before we even think about anything else. If that deepest need of our souls is not filled by God, we will waste our lives trying to fill it with anything and everything else. If you are not a Christian and have made it this far in the book, first of all, the fact that you read on despite the many references to Jesus might be proof that there is a God calling out to you. (Or you are truly my friend.) Second, if you didn't make your decision yet, I want to give you another opportunity here to make your relationship with God right. It starts with responding to the call of our shepherd, Jesus, receiving Him as Lord so that our sins may be forgiven and our relationship with God restored.

If you are a Christian, you didn't just waste two minutes reading the gospel message again. We must remind ourselves daily of our need for Jesus, not just for our salvation, but for our day-to-day sanctification to become more like Him. It is by grace we are able to choose God every day, say "no" to the desires of our flesh, and stand up against the attacks of Satan. It is by grace that even our good deeds and acts of service do not become for us ways in which we try to save ourselves.

God's grace should blow us away. He doesn't just forgive us of our sins and credit to us the full righteousness of His Son Jesus only to make us His little slaves in His kingdom. Even if He did do just that, we would count ourselves unworthy of such a title. We would still rejoice and sing His praise for eternity. Instead of slaves, though, God adopts us as His sons and daughters, making us heirs of God and co-heirs with His only begotten Son Jesus. If that's not enough, He then invites us to take part in what He is doing here on earth, empowering us with the Holy Spirit to do His kingdom work.

Escape from Alcatraz

Priscilla and I went to San Francisco shortly after we got married to visit some friends, and while we were there we did the Alcatraz tour. If you don't know what Alcatraz is, then you probably live under a rock (pun definitely intended). *The Rock* happens to be one of my favorite movies so I wanted to visit the prison in order to re-enact my favorite scenes in my mind. Unfortunately, all those areas were closed off to the public but the tour was worth it, nonetheless. Priscilla probably wouldn't have let me make a scene anyway.

Alcatraz is a really fascinating place. Apparently, it was a fort and arsenal during the Civil War and later turned into a prison. During the tour, they told these great stories of the different escape attempts. The guided audio tour also talked about what daily life was like for the prisoners. It was a highly regimented schedule, something like 6:30 a.m. wake-up until 9:30 p.m. lights out. Meals had to be taken at set times. The prisoners were put to work during the day, and if you were good you got some recreation time. And then repeat, day after day. One prisoner wrote that one of the hardest things about being in Alcatraz was the tedium, boredom, and lack of purpose. You just did the same things over and over again. Can you imagine life like that? Ten years . . . fifteen years . . . or however long you were sentenced for, doing the same things day in and day out?

I thought about that a bit and realized that we feel that way sometimes, don't we? We aren't in prison, but sometimes it feels like we're in this purposeless, endless cycle. We get up early each day to go to school or to work (6:30 a.m. actually sounds pretty good for some of us). Some of us wish we could go to bed at 9:30 p.m. But we have homework, tests, deadlines, or projects to do. We stress out but manage to get through them, only to face another round the next week. I've taken so many standardized tests that it is ridiculous. We look forward to certain things like the weekends to sleep in and do something fun, or vacation, but those come and go, and it's back to the routine drag of life. It feels like we are just digging holes, only to have them filled in at the end of the day, and having to start over the next day . . . and the next.

As Christians, we wish we could say that our life experience was different. If we are honest, though, most professing Christians would say that tedium and monotony is their daily experience rather than the streams of living water and life to the full that the Bible talks about. Whether or not you are a Christian, everyone knows that life is more than just surviving, existing, and going through the motions. In Christ we have new life, but many believers walk around as if we were bound by chains and shackles. Instead of participating fully in the divine nature, we are all tempted to turn to earthly substitutes to find meaning and significance.

The entertainment industry makes a boatload of money because people want to be caught up in a greater story. We forget that we are in the daddy of all epic stories, a cosmic battle between good and evil. Ephesians 6:12-13 reminds us that "Our struggle is not against flesh and blood, but against the rulers, against the authorities, against the powers of this dark world and against the spiritual forces of evil in the heavenly realms. Therefore put on the full armor of God, so that when the day of evil comes, you may be able to stand your ground, and after you have done everything, to stand." Unfortunately, most people walk around without their armor and weapons while Satan and his forces are picking off people left and right.

The truth is that you don't have to be a great pastor, missionary, or an outspoken defender of the oppressed to be significant in God's eternal kingdom. Many of the commands in the Bible have to do simply with everyday living. The really cool part is that if we live life looking forward to Christ's return in a way that bears witness to the gospel, our day-to-day experience takes on eternal significance. For example, take a look at what Paul commanded Titus to teach to the different churches on Crete:

You must teach what is in accord with sound doctrine. Teach the older men to be temperate, worthy of respect, self-controlled, and sound in faith, in love and in endurance.

Likewise, teach the older women to be reverent in the way they live, not to be slanderers or addicted to much wine, but to teach what is good. Then they can train the younger women to love their husbands and children, to be self-controlled and pure, to be busy at home, to be kind, and to be subject to their husbands, so that no one will malign the word of God.

Similarly, encourage the young men to be self-controlled. In everything set them an example by doing what is good. In your teaching show integrity, seriousness and soundness of speech that cannot be condemned, so that those who oppose you may be ashamed because they have nothing bad to say about us.

Teach slaves to be subject to their masters in every-
thing, to try to please them, not to talk back to them,
and not to steal from them, but to show that they
can be fully trusted, so that in every way they will
make the teaching about God our Savior attractive
(Titus 2:1-10).

These were instructions for living for different
groups of people. There's nothing extraordinary about
these commands. Paul didn't say "Go conquer enemy
forces," or "Everyone become missionaries." He told
older men to be temperate and worthy of respect, older
women to teach younger women to be kind to their husbands, younger men to be self-controlled, and slaves to
do their job well. These were instructions on how to live
an ordinary life.

But notice why they ought to do these ordinary
things, and do them well:

> ➢ So that God's Word would not be maligned;

> ➢ So that no one could have anything bad to
>   say against them;

> ➢ So the teachings of Christ might be made
>   attractive.

Simply living a life of godliness in their everyday life
had eternal impact because it gave testimony to the
gospel. Even slaves, in their service and bondage, had an

opportunity to make an impact of eternal significance in the way they served their masters.

Do you realize that the glory of God is at stake by the way you live? You bear witness to the gospel and bring glory to God when you show integrity with your homework, when you are patient with annoying people, when you honor your parents, when you don't cheat on your taxes, when you treat your sisters with purity, when you say no to pornography or to gossip, when you grow in qualities that will make you a good husband, or wife, or father, or mother, and when your marriage doesn't end in divorce. In all these things, realize that God's glory is on the line, because the opposite is sadly true. You malign God and His Word, and we actually move non-believers closer to hell, when we live self-centered, pointless lives. There are no such things as ordinary days. Every day is a chance to make a difference.

> The truth is that all of us, Christians or not, are worshippers. We all give our hearts to something. If not God, then it will be something else.

Even if we have our dream jobs, if we fix our eyes here on this earth and remain short-sighted, our daily lives will become tedious and without purpose. When we start looking around instead of at God, the grass starts looking greener everywhere else. The promise of the resurrection is that there is more to this life than what the eyes can see. There is an eternity, and my mundane living, if I am being daily sanctified towards godliness, can have an eternal impact in God's ultimate kingdom-advancing plan.

Jesus, in the Great Commission, sent us into the world to make disciples, to partner with God in advancing His kingdom here on earth. Part of the partnership is simply living in obedience in our daily routine, desiring to make the gospel attractive to those around us. Some of us, though, have been given more, whether it is intelligence, influence, resources, or skills. If we are in medicine, then we potentially have all of those things. We have an opportunity to advance God's kingdom in a way that many cannot and, in turn, to experience God in a way we can never imagine. Or we can build for ourselves a little kingdom here on earth which, like castles in the sand, will be simply lost to the wind and the waves of time.

Worth the Cost

Thirty some years ago, Rob and Mary Ann, new grads and newly-weds, decided to move to the West Coast because of a job opportunity. Rob had tremendous skill and experience even as a new graduate, having worked under Buckminster Fuller. I am convinced that he is a genius, although he would never admit it. (He has mathematical models hanging in his house as decoration.) He has had an accomplished career as an engineer. Still, with his talent, he could have done much better in his field, except he and his wife decided to invest in ministry. He eventually became an elder at our church and, with Mary Ann, committed to overseeing the youth group.

For the past two-plus decades, they have given themselves to the Lord and to the kids of the church. They affectionately are known as Uncle Rob and Auntie Mary Ann. Mary Ann laid aside her career in interior design in order to shape inner hearts instead. She would drive all around to round up kids for Bible study, a meal, or to go to church. Auntie Mary Ann would faithfully call me to pray in high school, even though that was the last thing I wanted to do. Uncle Rob poured into our lives, leading us on retreats, teaching us the Word, and eventually training us up to continue the ministry work. He even enrolled in seminary, and is set to complete his MDiv after ten years of part-time study amidst full-time work and church service (talk about dedication).

Of course that decision came with a cost. They set aside their own goals and ambitions. They stayed in the same small apartment and Rob drove his 1986 Camry to three hundred thousand plus miles until it finally died in recent years. In the eyes of the world, this was foolishness. What do they have to show for so many years of hard work and self-sacrifice? Not much in terms of wealth and worldly prestige, that's for sure.

I can think of perhaps a few things worth more than a nice house and a big savings account: two missionaries, a full-time pastor, and one confused doctor/church leader/writer just for starters. Not to mention a host of dedicated Christians who have come out of the youth group who are in nursing, pharmacy, engineering, real estate, teaching, finance, and film to name a few. This simple engineer and interior designer have impacted nearly every aspect of society.

Uncle Rob and Auntie Mary Ann, to all those who have said (or thought) this was a wasted life, to all the lies of Satan causing you to doubt the sacrifices you have made, I want to say your spiritual legacy will carry on well beyond any worldly gains. There are treasures awaiting that no moth and rust will destroy nor thieves break in to steal.

My life would be in a very dark place without Christ. Perhaps God would have saved me through other means if you had not given yourselves to the ministry. But God used you because you said yes to God's will over your own. Thank you for your unwavering faithfulness over the many, often thankless, years. It has not been a wasted life. It has been worth the cost. We love you.

Wrapping it Up

Until we get on board with God's salvation plan, we are going to miss out on the full life that Jesus makes available. God created each one of us uniquely and gifted us with different abilities and talents to serve Him. Whether God has one specific will for our lives, or we are automatically in God's will if we walk in obedience and faithfully use our gifts in whatever we are doing, I am not entirely sure. What I am sure of is that it is God's will to advance His kingdom here on earth, preparing the world for Christ's return when all will be brought under the reign of God.

That the Bible has made clear, and we would do well to at least get that part right.

What I hoped to accomplish in this book was to remind you (as well as myself) that, as Christians, our comfort and security are not God's primary concerns. Yet, by the way some professing Christians live and how they spend their resources, time, and energy, the world may think that our earthly well-being is God's top priority. Those who live simply for themselves, chasing after the empty promises of this world, will have a rude awakening in store when they come before God to give an account for what He has given them.

I'm not trying to bring a message of doom and gloom. But the reality is, in anything you choose to do (but in my biased opinion particularly in medicine because of what it demands), if Jesus is not functionally Lord in your life, the best case scenario is that you will side-track your calling, and what you build on this life will be with straw, wood, and hay that will be burned up while you barely escape the flames (1 Corinthians 3:15). At the very worst, you might find at the end of your life that because Jesus was not really Lord, there will not be entry into God's eternal kingdom (Matthew 7:21-23).

We are created for far more than simple existence. Let's not settle for the ordinary. Let's not settle for counterfeits of the extra-ordinary, filling our lives with movies, games, and other temporary forms of entertainment. As Christians we are called to embrace life that really is life, and that means getting on board with what God is doing here on earth.

Someone once said, "Find a job you love and you'll never have to work a day in your life."[37] You might find a job you love and have a pretty good life, but that would mean nothing if it is done apart from God. What good will it be, indeed, for a man if he gains the whole world, but forfeits his soul? I say, "Keep Jesus your first love and God's kingdom your first priority, and it will be worth the cost whatever you do." Not as catchy, I know. But that was the best I could do.

Reflection Questions

1. What things or activities give you a sense of purpose and meaning?

2. Do you feel stuck running an endless race? How does Jesus' death on the cross change the mundane things of everyday life?

3. According to the Bible, what has God been doing throughout history? How much of what you are doing is aligned with God's purposes in this world?

Afterword

WELL, THERE YOU HAVE IT, THE SUM TOTAL OF ALL my wisdom and experience. Please give me your feedback on what was helpful, what wasn't, what you would like to know more about, or even just how you interacted with the book.

I would love to hear how God has moved in your life and where He is taking you. If you would like to contact me, e-mail me at: *jacktsai@unfailingspring.com*. Or visit my website and you can leave me a message: *www.unfailingspring.com*.

You might be thinking, *Gosh Jack, this is all kind of radical. How can I be sure you know what you are talking about?*

Trust me. I'm a doctor, after all.

Appendix

Practical Tips for Those Going into Medicine

A SIDE FROM ALL THE SPIRITUAL THINGS, I DID WANT to offer some helpful tips about the various stages of your journey, if medicine is where God has called you to. I have categorized them by different periods of training, but most of them transcend such boundaries.

High School

Develop photographic memory. This will make your life a lot easier. If that's not possible, see below.

Memorize Scripture. Or memorize anything else that you are interested in like songs, poems, or movie lines. This is a great way to exercise your brain. It will make memorizing the Kreb cycle much easier later, trust me.[38] Plus, it helps during medical training when you don't have time to do your quiet time or you have nothing to do while you stand in the operating room retracting the bladder blade for six hours.

Read books. I wish I had read much more when I had more time. And not just fun novels but non-fiction books too. Not only do you become more knowledgeable and interesting, but it also helps you write better.

Learn Spanish. This is especially key if you want to practice in California and not want to cut your head off having to use the interpreter phone every time.

Talk to as many doctors, residents, and med students as you can. Get their perspective on what they love and especially what they hate about medicine.

Don't procrastinate! I hate to say this, but yes you do have to get good grades to get into medical school. Do you have to get straight A's? No, but all B's and C's isn't going to cut it, either. Develop good studying skills. If you can be disciplined and do a little work and study every day, then college will be a piece of cake. (Or easier, at least.)

Grow a sense of humor. Medicine is a long road. You are going to hate life at times and there will be people who will make you hate life even more. It helps to be able to laugh at yourself or the situation (or the person yelling at you—in your head, of course, not out loud!). Some situations you simply can't control.

If you didn't get the point yet, learn humility. This is a must have and we need as much time as we can to develop it. You might be the star student in high school and college but once you hit medical school, you will not automatically be at the top of the class anymore. Learn early that you don't know everything, and learn to learn from everyone.

Please work on your social skills. I am by no means the coolest guy you have hung out with, but I like to think I can carry on a normal conversation. You will have to interact with people, including people not in your field, no matter what field you go to. Ultimately, people get hired not because they are necessarily the smartest or the best, but if they can get along with others. PS. Studying all the time doesn't help this.

Be a patient. As a future medical provider, it helps to know what patients go through when they get sick. If you are blessed with great health, make sure you at least spend time with patients and talk to them about their experiences.

College

You don't have to be some sort of science major to apply to medical school. On the flip side, don't shy away from a science major that you are interested in because all the pre-meds are that major and it's too competitive. Do what you are interested in and you will probably get better grades. You will have more pre-requisite classes to take, though, if you choose a non-science major.

There is no requirement that everyone needs to do re-search, volunteer, and be the president of multiple charity clubs. Do a few things well, things about which you can feel and talk passionately.

It is never too late to apply to medical school if that's where God is calling you, even if you are already working in a completely different field.

Apply again even if you don't get in the first time, if this is where you feel God is leading you. Maybe the timing was not right and God wanted to grow you during the time you have to wait. If the doors close many times, though, you might consider this as God's way of saying, "Choose another career path."

Learn about the healthcare system. Our system is majorly complex. We don't need to be experts in it, but it helps to understand how our system works and what the needs are. Understanding other healthcare systems and how we compare is a plus during interviews.

Develop your teaching skills. As a doctor, you are not just a life-long learner, but a teacher as well. Learn to explain things simply, as you will be educating patients, your colleagues, residents, and medical students for the rest of your career.

If possible, travel. This will make you more interesting during interviews. Depending on where you go, traveling might help you to appreciate all that you have.

Medical School

Prioritize. Make a list before medical school of what is absolutely important to you, whether it be hobbies, God, or relationships. There is just too much to learn in medicine. Take it from one who knows, you will never feel like you studied enough because there is always more to know. Put in your due effort, but at some point you'll need to set your boundaries and make time for the things you can't live without.

Don't buy an ophthalmoscope. Unless ophthalmology is your thing or you are actively involved in street medicine, you probably won't need one. They are really expensive and most clinics you go to have them in the rooms.

Learn to share. Help out your fellow classmates because you are all in the same boat. You never know who you will need a consult from later.

Journal. This can be quite therapeutic and, who knows, maybe someday you will write a book.

Exercise. And do it regularly. It gives you a break from your studying and you will feel better. Plus, you'll have a clear conscience when you tell your patients to exercise.

Do not study the day before your boards. If you do, you will fail. Okay, maybe not fail, but it's just not necessary. Relaxing and getting a good night's rest will serve you better than cramming any last minute details. I had a policy of not pulling all-nighters, and I did pretty well keeping that.

Talk with your classmates who have kids. They will teach you about perspective and priorities.

Be nice to the nurses! This goes for the rest of your career. They will rescue you when you have no idea what you are doing. You might even get in on their food.

Did I mention humility? Don't let pride go to your head, and you'll be a better doctor. If you don't know something, it's better to admit it. And if you need emotional support, don't be too prideful to seek it out.

How should you choose your residency? Ask different physicians what they see the majority of the time in their practice. You might dream of doing amazing surgeries, but a lot of general surgeons spend a lot of time taking out appendixes and gallbladders. You might love figuring out kidney problems, but nephrologists often deal mostly with dialysis. Find out what the bread and butter of each specialty is, and ask if you could see yourself enjoying doing that day after day.

Develop your lifelines. These are the things that renew, encourage, and support you that you probably neglected throughout medical school. Fourth year after residency interviews is a great time to re-establish these in your life. Most important are your relationship with God and others, but other lifelines include your hobbies and passions outside of medicine.

Residency

DO NOT LIE. If your senior resident or attending asks if you did something but you forgot, say you forgot. Do not say that you did it, and certainly do not make up anything. Eventually you will get burned.

Do not go to the gym in your scrubs. You might have forgotten your gym clothes, but it just looks like you are trying to show off.

Reread your personal statement. Break out your personal statement from time to time. Your interests or vision may change, but it is good to remind yourself of your initial convictions.

Have sign-out parties. We would get together as a class right before rotations switched to give each other hints of what to watch out for in the upcoming rotation. It was also nice to vent once in awhile and know there are others going through similar experiences.

Take time-outs. As an intern you'll be running around like a headless chicken, rushing from floor to floor, patient room to patient room. Sometimes you just need to mentally check out for a moment. There was this place outside the hospital I would go to from time to time just to regroup. Even if you can't escape, pausing for thirty seconds before seeing the next patient can help catch your emotions up to your body so that you can be fully present.

Learn your patients' names. It's amazing how there are days I can't remember a single name of the patients I saw that day. Sometimes we emotionally distance ourselves from patients because the work is hard and it's painful if patients don't do well. But I think it is this dehumanization that makes our job seem pointless and futile. Our patients become just another thing to fix, another obstacle asking for our energy and time, both of which are already so limited. But connecting with patients as people can help us celebrate the small victories even if there's no ultimate cure for what they have.

Don't be afraid to make mistakes. Volunteer to do the thing you are most afraid to do. Sign up to teach the topic you don't understand. Your job as a resident is to learn; you are even expected to make mistakes. It might be embarrassing to admit you don't know something. It'll be worse when you are a senior resident not knowing something you should have learned as an intern because you never asked about it or tried it.

Don't hold your pee. Go if you have to.

Acknowledgments

IF YOU WERE TO SOMEHOW TELL ME AT THE END OF HIGH school that I would be playing doctor, pastor, and writer in ten years, I would tell you in no uncertain terms that you were out of your mind. It has been such an incredible journey ever since I accepted Christ as Lord, so first and foremost, thank you God for pouring out grace undeserving.

To my church family at SBECC, thank you for walking with me every step of the way, guiding and protecting, nurturing and encouraging me toward more Christ-like-ness. There are so many amazing memories. Uncle Rob, Auntie Mary Ann, and Auntie Helen, may God keep you faithful until the very end.

Thank you to those who reviewed the manuscript. Sorry that I can't mention everyone by name, but in particular, I would like to recognize Brian Li and Jesse Chou, who were so thorough in their feedback. You will make fantastic doctors. (Jesse, it is not too late to come to the dark side.) Also, thank you Madeline Wu for reviewing the final draft.

Of course, without the influence and life example of Dr. Nick, I would not have stepped out in faith. Thank you. To David Biebel, who God sovereignly provided to edit and publish this book, I appreciate all that you have done to make this process easier and the book better. I also want to thank all my patients who have taught me more than I could ever learn from reading a textbook. You all have been so gracious.

To my parents and my brother, you have always been there for me. May you come to know the Lord soon.

Finally, a big thank you to my beautiful wife and precious co-heir with Christ. Priscilla, I love you with all that I know how. I pray that God will continue to teach me to love you even more as we walk this journey together, until death do us part, or Jesus Christ returns.

Bibliography

Arnold, Clinton E. *Ephesians*. Grand Rapids, Mich.: Zondervan, 2010.

Bock, Darrell L. *Luke*. Grand Rapids, Mich.: Baker Academic, 1994.

Christian Community Health Fellowship, http://www.cchf.org.

Christian Medical & Dental Associations, http://www.cmda.org.

Cho, Joohee. "Game Addicts Arrested for Starving Baby to Death." *ABC News*, March 4, 2010. Accessed Feb. 9, 2013. http://abcnews.go.com/International/TheLaw/baby-death-alleged-result-parents-online-games-addiction/story?id=10007040#.ULD9l2eEvE0.

Coe, John. "The Seven Deadly Disconnects of Seminary Training: Theological and Spiritual Formation Reflections on a Transformation Model." ETS 2005 Paper Proposal, 2005.

Draper, Charles W., Chad Brand, and Archie England, eds. *Holman Illustrated Bible Dictionary*. Revised ed. Nashville, TN: Holman Reference, 2003.

Fee, Gordon D. *Paul's Letter to the Philippians*. Grand Rapids, Mich.: Wm. B. Eerdmans Publishing Company, 1995.

Health Steward, http://www.healthstewards.com.

Joint Commission, the, Standards and Information, http://www.jointcommission.org.

Kairo English Ministry, South Bay Evangelical Christian Church, http://kairo.sbecc.org.

Krupa, Caroyne. "Medical Students Still Burdened by High Debt Loads." *amednews.com*, Aug. 27, 2012. Accessed Feb. 10, 2013. http://www.ama-assn.org/amednews/2012/08/27/prsb0827.htm.

Leclerc, Philip. *Divided*, the movie. National Center for Family-Integrated Churches, 2011. http://dividedthemovie.com.

Medical Strategic Network, the, www.gomets.org.

MedSend, http://www.medsend.org.

Murphy SL, et al. "Deaths: Preliminary Data for 2010." *National Vital Statistics Reports*, 2012 January 11; Vol 60, No 4.

National Health Service Corps, http://www.nhsc.hrsa.gov/scholarships/overview/index.html.

Noonan, David. "Doctors Who Kill Themselves." *The Daily Beast*, April 19, 2008. Accessed Feb 9, 2013. http://www.thedailybeast.com/newsweek/2008/04/19/doctors-who-kill-themselves.html.

Patrick, Dr. John, http://www.johnpatrick.ca. Speeches. Christian Medical and Dental Association.

Platt, David. *Radical: Taking Your Back Your Faith From the American Dream*. Colorado Springs: Multnomah Books, 2010.

Saguil A, Phelps K. "The Spiritual Assessment." *American Family Physician*, September 15, 2012.

Shanafelt TD, et al. "Burnout and Satisfaction With Work-Life Balance Among US Physicians Relative to the General US Population." *Archives of Internal Medicine*, August 20, 2012.

Unfailing Spring, www.unfailingspring.com.

Waltke, Bruce K. with Fredricks, Cathi J. *Genesis: a Commentary*, Grand Rapids, Mich.: Zondervan, 2001.

World Health Organization, Commission on Social Determinants of Health, Marmot, Sir Michael, Chair.

World Harvest Mission, http://www.whm.org.

Yarnell KS, et al. "Primary Care: Is There Enough Time for Prevention." *American Journal of Public Health*, April 2003.

Notes

[1] Speaking of disclosures, no pharmaceutical company paid for the writing of this book so we're good.

[2] Besides his dedication to serve the poor, Dr. Nick has an amazing testimony of his own spiritual journey to wellness. Check out his ministry at http://www.healthstewards.com.

[3] Come visit! http://kairo.sbecc.org.

[4] Darrell L. Bock, *Luke* (Grand Rapids, Mich.: Baker Academic, 1994), 1284-1287.

[5] Caroyne Krupa, "Medical Students Still Burdened by High Debt Loads," *amednews.com*, Aug. 27, 2012, accessed May 2, 2013, http://bit.ly/13QFqTm.

[6] Bruce K. Waltke with Cathi J. Fredricks, *Genesis: a Commentary* (Grand Rapids, Mich.: Zondervan, 2001), 178-184.

[7] Bock, *Luke*, 1146-1155.

[8] David Platt, *Radical: Taking Back Your Faith From the American Dream* (Colorado Springs: Multnomah Books, 2010), 6-13.

[9] David Noonan, "Doctors Who Kill Themselves," *The Daily Beast*, April 19, 2008, accessed May 3, 2013, http://thebea.st/NbO36L.

[10] Charles W. Draper, Chad Brand, and Archie England, eds., *Holman Illustrated Bible Dictionary*, Revised ed. (Nashville, TN: Holman Reference, 2003), 1025.

[11] Yarnell KS, et al., "Primary Care: Is There Enough Time for Prevention," *American Journal of Public Health*, 2003 April; 93 (4): 635-41.

[12] Shanafelt TD, et al., "Burnout and Satisfaction With Work-Life Balance Among US Physicians Relative to the General US Population," *Archives of Internal Medicine*, 2012 Aug 20:1-9.

[13] Murphy SL, et al., "Deaths: Preliminary Data for 2010," *National Vital Statistics Reports*, 2012 January 11; Vol 60, No 4.

[14] I first heard much of this from a talk by Dr. John Patrick, who speaks for the Christian Medical and Dental Associations.

[15] Gordon D. Fee, *Paul's Letter to the Philippians* (Grand Rapids, Mich.: Wm. B. Eerdmans Publishing Company, 1995), 305-325.

[16] See research by Sir Michael Marmot, Chair of the Commission on Social Determinants of Health (World Health Organization).

[17] DKA stands for diabetic ketoacidosis, a potentially life-threatening complication of uncontrolled diabetes. Osteomyelitis is an infection involving the bone.

[18] A summary of data can be found in this article: Saguil A, Phelps K., "The Spiritual Assessment," *American Family Physician*, Sept. 15, 2012; 86 (6):546-550.

[19] "Standards FAQ Details," last modified November 24, 2008, accessed May 3, 2013, http://bit.ly/106903j.

[20] http://www.gomets.org/student_project.html.

[21] www.cchf.org.

[22] www.cmda.org.

[23] John Coe, "The Seven Deadly Disconnects of Seminary Training: Theological and Spiritual Formation Reflections on a Transformation Model" (ETS 2005 Paper Proposal, 2005), 1-3.

[24] This verse is the inspiration for my website www.unfailingspring.com. Please visit!

[25] Dr. Carlan Wendler is currently serving with World Harvest Mission in Burundi. In addition to patient care, he will be training native physicians at a local medical school. If you would like more info, visit http://www.whm.org.

[26] Clinton E. Arnold, *Ephesians* (Grand Rapids, Mich.: Zondervan, 2010), 204-225.

[27] Arnold, *Ephesians*, 413-416.

[28] John Coe, "Spiritual Theology: A Theological-experiential Methodology for Bridging the Sanctification Gap," *Journal of Spiritual Formation & Soul Care* Vol. 2, No. 1 (2009): 24.

[29] Arnold, *Ephesians*, 428-429.

[30] Arnold, *Ephesians*, 418-419.

[31] http://dividedthemovie.com.

[32] Bock, *Luke*, 1156-1169.

[33] Big seminary word! Biblical hermeneutics is just the science of interpreting Scripture.

[34] http://www.nhsc.hrsa.gov/scholarships/overview/index.html.

[35] www.medsend.org.

[36] Joohee Cho, "Game Addicts Arrested for Starving Baby to Death," *ABC News*, March 4, 2010, accessed May 3, 2013, http://abcn.ws/16wkR2K.

[37] According to my very extensive research on the Internet, it was either author Jim Fox or Confucius.

[38] I've been picking on the Kreb cycle a lot. It's the only thing I can remember from organic chemistry.

RESOURCES FROM HEALTHY LIFE PRESS

We've Got Mail: The New Testament Letters in Modern English – As Relevant Today as Ever! by Rev. Warren C. Biebel, Jr. – A modern English paraphrase of the New Testament Letters, sure to inspire in readers a loving appreciation for God's Word. (Printed book: $9.95; PDF eBook: $6.95; both together: $15.00, direct from publisher; eBook reader versions available at *www.Amazon.com*; *www.BN.com*; *www.eChristian.com*.)

Hearth & Home – Recipes for Life, by Karey Swan (7th Edition) – Far more than a cookbook, this classic is a life book, with recipes for life as well as for great food. Karey describes how to buy and prepare from scratch a wide variety of tantalizing dishes, while weaving into  the book's fabric the wisdom of the ages plus the recipe that she and her husband used to raise their kids. A great gift for Christmas or for a new bride. (Perfect Bound book [8 x 10, glossy cover]: $17.95; PDF eBook: $12.95; both together: $24.95, direct from publisher; eBook reader versions available at *www.Amazon.com*; *www.BN.com*; *www.eChristian.com*.)

Who Me, Pray? Prayer 101: Praying Aloud, for Beginners, by Gary A. Burlingame – Who Me, Pray? is a practical guide for prayer, based on Jesus' direction in "The Lord's Prayer," with examples provided for use in typical situations where you might be asked or expected to pray in public. (Printed book: $6.95; PDF eBook: $2.99; both together: $7.95, direct from publisher; eBook reader versions available at *www.Amazon.com*; *www.BN.com*; *www.eChristian.com*.)

The Big Black Book – What the Christmas Tree Saw, by Rev. Warren C. Biebel, Jr. – An original Christmas story, from the perspective of the Christmas tree. This little book is especially suitable for parents to read to their children at Christmas time or all year-round. (**Full-color printed book**: $9.95; PDF eBook: $4.95; both together: $10.95, direct from publisher; eBook reader versions available at *www.Amazon.com*; *www.BN.com*; *www.eChristian.com*.)

My Broken Heart Sings, the poetry of Gary Burlingame – In 1987, Gary and his wife Debbie lost their son Christopher John, at only six months of age, to a chronic lung disease. This life-changing experience gave them a special heart for helping others through similar loss and pain. (Printed book: $10.95; PDF eBook: $6.95; both together: $13.95; eBook reader versions available at *www.Amazon.com*; *www.BN.com*; *www.eChristian.com*.)

After Normal: One Teen's Journey Following Her Brother's Death, by Diane Aggen – Based on a journal the author kept following her younger brother's death. It offers helpful insights and understanding for teens facing a similar loss or for those who might wish to understand and help teens facing a similar loss. (Printed book: $11.95; PDF eBook: $6.95; both together: $15.00; eBook reader versions available at *www.Amazon.com*; *www.BN.com*; *www.eChristian.com*.)

In the Unlikely Event of a Water Landing – Lessons Learned from Landing in the Hudson River, by Andrew Jamison, MD – The author was flying standby on US Airways Flight 1549 toward Charlotte on January 15, 2009, from New York City, where he had been inter-

viewing for a residency position. Little did he know that the next stop would be the Hudson River. Riveting and inspirational, this book would be especially helpful for people in need of hope and encouragement. (Printed book: $8.95; PDF eBook: $6.95; both together: $12.95, direct from publisher; eBook reader versions available at *www.Amazon.com*; *www.BN.com*; *www.eChristian.com.*)

 **Finding Martians in the Dark – Everything I Needed to Know About Teaching Took Me Only 30 Years to Learn**, by Dan M. Biebel – Packed with wise advice based on hard experience, and laced with humor, this book is a perfect teacher's gift year-round. Susan J. Wegmann, PhD, says, "Biebel's sardonic wit is mellowed by a genuine love for kids and teaching. . . . A Whitman-like sensibility flows through his stories of teaching, learning, and life." (Printed book: $10.95; PDF eBook: $6.95; Together: $15.00; eBook reader versions available at *www. Amazon.com*; *www. BN.com*; *www.eChristian.com.*)

Because We're Family and **Because We're Friends**, by Gary A. Burlingame – Sometimes things related to faith can be hard to discuss with your family and friends. These booklets are designed to be   given as gifts, to help you open the door to discussing spiritual matters with family members and friends who are open to such a conversation. (Printed book: $5.95 each; PDF eBook: $4.95 each; both together: $9.95 [printed & eBook of the same title], direct from publisher; eBook reader versions available at *www.Amazon.com*; *www. BN.com*; *www.eChristian.com.*)

The Transforming Power of Story: How Telling Your Story Brings Hope to Others and Healing to Yourself, by Elaine Leong Eng, MD, and David B. Biebel, DMin – This book demonstrates, through multiple true life stories, how sharing one's story, especially in a group setting, can bring hope to listeners and healing to the one who shares. Individuals facing difficulties will find this book greatly encouraging. (Printed book: $14.99; PDF eBook: $9.99; both together: $19.99, direct from publisher; eBook reader versions available at *www.Amazon.com*; *www. BN.com*; *www.eChristian.com*.)

You Deserved a Better Father: Good Parenting Takes a Plan, by Robb Brandt, MD – About parenting by intention, and other lessons the author learned through the loss of his firstborn son. It is especially for parents who believe that bits and pieces of leftover time will be enough for their own children. (Printed book: $10.95

each; PDF eBook: $6.95; both together: $12.95, direct from publisher; eBook reader versions available at *www.Amazon. com*; *www.BN.com*; *www.eChristian.com*.)

Jonathan, You Left Too Soon, by David B. Biebel, DMin – One pastor's journey through the loss of his son, into the darkness of depression, and back into the light of joy again, emerging with a renewed sense of mission. (Printed book: $12.95; PDF eBook: $5.99; both together: $15.00, direct from publisher; eBook reader versions available at *www.Amazon.com*; *www.BN.com*; *www.eChristian.com*.)

If God Is So Good, Why Do I Hurt So Bad?, by David B. Biebel, DMin – In this best-selling classic (over 200,000 copies in print worldwide, in five languages) on the subject of loss and renewal, first published in 1989, the author comes alongside people in pain, and shows the way through and beyond it, to joy again. This book has proven helpful to those who are struggling and to those who wish to understand and help. (Printed book: $12.95; PDF eBook: $8.95; both together: $19.95, direct from publisher; eBook reader versions available at *www.Amazon.com*; *www.BN.com*; *www.eChristian.com*.)

The Spiritual Fitness Checkup for the 50-Something Woman, by Sharon V. King, PhD – Following the stages of a routine medical exam, the author describes ten spiritual fitness "check-ups" midlife women can conduct to assess their spiritual health and tone up their relationship with God. Each checkup consists of the author's  personal reflections, a Scripture reference for meditation, and a "Spiritual Pulse Check," with exercises readers can use for personal application. (Printed book: $8.95; PDF eBook: $6.95; both together: $12.95, direct from publisher; eBook reader versions available at *www.Amazon.com*; *www.BN.com*; *www. eChristian.com*.)

The Other Side of Life – Over 60? God Still Has a Plan for You, by Rev. Warren C. Biebel, Jr. – Drawing on biblical examples and his 60-plus years of pastoral experience, Rev. Biebel helps older (and younger) adults understand God's view of aging and the rich life available to everyone who seeks a deeper relationship with God as they age. Rev. Biebel explains how to: Identify God's ongoing plan for your life; Rely on faith to manage the anxieties of aging; Form positive, supportive relationships; Cultivate patience; Cope with new technologies; Develop spiritual integrity; Understand the effects of dementia; Develop a

Christ-centered perspective of aging. (Printed book: $10.95; PDF eBook: $6.95; both together: $15.00, direct from publisher; eBook reader versions available at *www.Amazon.com*; *www.BN.com*; *www.eChristian.com*.)

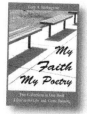

My Faith, My Poetry, by Gary A. Burlingame – This unique book of Christian poetry is actually two in one. The first collection of poems, A Day in the Life, explores a working parent's daily journey of faith. The reader is carried from morning to bedtime, from "In the Details," to "I Forgot to Pray," back to "Home Base," and finally to "Eternal Love Divine." The second collection of poems, Come Running, is wonder, joy, and faith wrapped up in words that encourage and inspire the mind and the heart. (Printed book: $10.95; PDF eBook: $6.95; both together: $13.95, direct from publisher; eBook reader versions available at *www.Amazon.com*; *www.BN.com*; *www.eChristian.com*.)

On Eagles' Wings, by Sara Eggleston – One woman's life journey from idyllic through chaotic to joy, carried all the way by the One who has promised to never leave us nor forsake us. Remarkable, poignant, moving, and inspiring, this autobiographical account will help many who are facing difficulties that seem too great to overcome

or even bear at all. It is proof that Isaiah 40:31 is as true today as when it was penned, "But they that wait upon the LORD shall renew their strength; they shall mount up with wings as eagles; they shall run, and not be weary; and they shall walk, and not faint." (Printed book: $14.95; PDF eBook: $8.95; both together: $22.95, direct from publisher; eBook reader versions available at *www.Amazon.com*; *www.BN.com*; *www.eChristian.com*.)

Richer Descriptions, by Gary A. Burlingame – A unique and handy manual, covering all nine human senses in seven chapters, for Christian speakers and writers. Exercises and a speaker's checklist equip speakers to engage their audiences in a richer experience. Writing examples and a writer's guide help writers bring more life to the characters and scenes of their stories. Bible references encourage a deeper appreciation of being created by God for a sensory existence. (Printed book: $15.95; PDF eBook: $8.95; both together: $22.95, direct from publisher; eBook reader versions available at *www.Amazon.com*; *www.BN.com*; *www. eChristian.com*.)

Treasuring Grace, by Rob Plumley and Tracy Roberts – This novel was inspired by a dream. Liz Swanson's life isn't quite what she'd imagined, but she considers herself lucky. She has a good husband, beautiful children, and fulfillment outside of her home through volunteer work. On some days she doesn't even notice the  dull ache in her heart. While she's preparing for their summer kickoff at Lake George, the ache disappears and her sudden happiness is mistaken for anticipation of their weekend. However, as the family heads north, there are clouds on the horizon that have nothing to do with the weather. Only Liz's daughter, who's found some of her mother's hidden journals, has any idea what's wrong. But by the end of the weekend, there will be no escaping the truth or its painful buried secrets. (Printed: $12.95; PDF eBook: $7.95; both together: $19.95, direct from publisher; eBook reader versions available at *www.Amazon.com*; *www.BN.com*; *www.eChristian.com*.)

Life's A Symphony, by Mary Z. Smith – When Kate Spence Cooper receives the news that her husband, Jack, has been killed in the war, she and her young son Jeremy move back to Crawford Wood, Tennessee to be closer to family. Since Jack's death Kate feels that she's lost trust in everyone, including God. Will she ever find her way back to the only One whom she can always depend upon? And what about Kate's match making brother, Chance? The cheeky man has other ideas on how to bring happiness into his sister's life once more. (Printed book: $12.95; PDF eBook: $7.95; both together: $19.95, direct from publisher; eBook reader versions available at *www.Amazon.com*; *www.BN.com*; *www.eChristian.com*.)

From Orphan to Physician – The Winding Path, by Chun-Wai Chan, MD – From the foreword: "In this book, Dr. Chan describes how his family escaped to Hong Kong, how they survived in utter poverty, and how he went from being an orphan to graduating from Harvard Medical School and becoming a cardiologist.  The writing is fluent, easy to read and understand. The sequence of events is realistic, emotionally moving, spiritually touching, heart-warming, and thought provoking. The book illustrates . . . how one must have faith in order to walk through life's winding path." (Printed book: $14.95; PDF eBook: $8.95; both together: $22.95, direct from publisher; eBook reader versions available at *www.Amazon.com*; *www.BN.com*; *www.eChristian.com*.)

12 Parables, by Wayne Faust – Timeless Christian stories about doubt, fear, change, grief, and more. Using tight, entertaining prose, professional musician and comedy performer Wayne Faust manages to deal with difficult concepts in a simple, straightforward way. These are stories you can read aloud over and over—to your spouse, your family, or in a group setting. Packed with emotion and just enough mystery to keep you wondering, while providing lots of points to ponder and discuss when you're through, these stories relate the gospel in the tradition of the greatest speaker of parables the world has ever known, who appears in them often. (Printed book: $14.95; PDF eBook: $8.95; both together: $22.95, direct from publisher; eBook reader versions available at *www.Amazon.com*; *www.BN.com*; *www.eChristian.com*.)

The Answer is Always "Jesus," by Aram Haroutunian, who gave children's sermons for 15 years at a large church in Golden, Colorado—well over 500 in all. This book contains 74 of his most unforgettable presentations—due to the children's responses. Pastors, homeschoolers, parents who often lead family devotions, or other storytellers will find these stories, along with comments about props and how to prepare and present them, an invaluable asset in reconnecting with the simplest, most profound truths of Scripture, and then to envision how best to communicate these so even a child can understand them. (Printed book: $12.95; PDF eBook: $8.95; both together: $19.95, direct from publisher; eBook reader versions available at *www.Amazon.com*; *www.BN.com*; *www.eChristian.com*.)

Handbook of Faith, by Rev. Warren C. Biebel, Jr. – The New York Times World 2011 Almanac claimed that there are 2 billion, 200 thousand Christians in the world, with "Christians" being defined as "followers of Christ." The original 12 followers of Christ changed the world; indeed, they changed the history of the world. So this 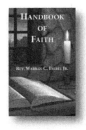 author, a pastor with over 60 years' experience, poses and answers this logical question: "If there are so many 'Christians' on this planet, why are they so relatively ineffective in serving the One they claim to follow?" Answer: Because, unlike Him, they do not know and trust the Scriptures, implicitly. This little volume will help you do that. (Printed book: $8.95; PDF eBook: $6.95; both together: $13.95, direct from publisher; eBook reader versions available at *www.Amazon.com*; *www.BN.com*; *www.eChristian.com*.)

Pieces of My Heart, by David L. Wood – Eighty-two lessons from normal everyday life. David's hope is that these stories will spark thoughts about God's constant involvement and intervention in our lives and stir a sense of how much He cares about every detail that is important to us. The piece missing represents his son, Daniel, who died in a fire shortly before his first birthday. (Printed book: $16.95; PDF eBook: $8.95; both together: $24.95, direct from publisher; eBook reader versions available at *www.Amazon.com*; *www.BN.com*; *www.eChristian.com*.)

> **NOTE:** *Pieces of My Heart is also available in two volumes. Vol. 1 is the first 39 chapters of this inspiring book; Vol. 2 is chapters 40-82 of the larger volume. Couples have enjoyed reading these two volumes concurrently, then discussing the great lessons they contain. (Each of these new volumes are $10.95 for the printed book, $6.95 for the PDF eBook version; both together: $14.95, direct from publisher; eBook reader versions available at www.Amazon.com; www.BN.com; www.eChristian.com.)*

Dream House, by Justa Carpenter – Written by a New England builder of several hundred homes, the idea for this book came to him one day as he was driving that came to him one day as was driving from one job site to another. He pulled over and recorded it so he would remember it, and now you will remember it, too, if you believe, as he does, that ". . . He who has begun a good work in you will complete it until the day of Jesus Christ." (Printed book: $8.95; PDF eBook: $6.95; both together: $13.95, direct from publisher; eBook reader versions available at *www.Amazon.com*; *www.BN.com*; *www.eChristian.com*.)

A Simply Homemade Clean, by homesteader Lisa Barthuly – "Somewhere along the path, it seems we've lost our gumption, the desire to make things ourselves," says the author. "Gone are the days of 'do it yourself.' Really . . . why bother? There are a slew of retailers just waiting for us with anything and everything we could need; packaged up all pretty, with no thought or effort required. It is the manifestation of 'progress' . . . right?" I don't buy that!" Instead, Lisa describes how to make safe and effective cleansers for home, laundry, and body right in your own home. This saves money and avoids exposure to harmful chemicals often found in commercially produced cleansers. (Printed book: $12.99; PDF eBook: $6.95; both together: $16.95, direct from publisher; **full-color printed book: $16.99, only at** *www.healthylifepress.com*; eBook reader versions available at *www.Amazon.com*; *www.BN.com*; *www.eChristian.com.*)

2013 TITLES

The Secret of Singing Springs, by Monte Swan – One Colorado family's treasure-hunting adventure along the trail of Jesse James. The Secret of Singing Springs is written to capture for children and their parents the spirit of the hunt—the hunt for treasure as in God's Truth, which is the objective of walking the Way of Wisdom that is described in Proverbs. (Printed book: $12.99; PDF eBook: $9.99; both together: $19.99, direct from publisher; eBook reader versions available at *www.Amazon.com*; *www.BN.com*; *www.eChristian.com.*)

God Loves You Circle, by Michelle Johnson – Daily inspiration for your deeper walk with Christ. This collection of short stories of Christian living will make you laugh, make you cry, but most of all make you contemplate—the meaning and value of walking with the Master moment-by-moment, day-by-day. (**Full-color printed book**: $17.95; full-color PDF eBook: $9.99; both together: $23.99, **only at *www.healthylifepress.com***; eBook reader versions available at *www.Amazon.com*; *www.BN.com*; *www.eChristian.com*.)

Our God Given Senses, by Gary A. Burlingame – Did you know humans have NINE senses? The Bible draws on these senses to reveal spiritual truth. We are to taste and see that the Lord is a good. We are to carry the fragrance of Christ. Our faith is produced upon hearing. Jesus asked Thomas to touch him. God created

us for a sensory experience and that is what you will find in this book. (Printed book: $12.99; PDF eBook: $9.99; both together: $19.99, direct from publisher; eBook reader versions available at *www.Amazon.com*; *www.BN.com*; *www.eChristian.com*.)

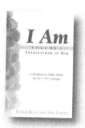

I AM – Transformed in Him (Volume 1) – by Diana Burg and Kim Tapfer, a meditative women's Bible study on the I AM statements of Christ in two 6-week volumes or one 12-week volume (12-week volume available 2014). Throughout this six week study you will begin to unearth the treasure trove of riches that are found within God's name, I AM WHO I AM. (Printed book: $12.99; PDF eBook: $9.99; both together: $19.99, direct from publisher; **COPIES OF VOLUME 1 AUTOGRAPHED BY BOTH AUTHORS ARE AVAILABLE FROM THE PUBLISHER, with free shipping: *www.healthylifepress.com*.** eBook reader versions available at *www.Amazon.com*; *www.BN.com*; *www.eChristian.com*.)

VOWS, a Romantic novel by F. F. Whitestone – When the police cruiser pulled up to the curb outside, Faith Framingham's heart skipped a beat, for she could see that Chuck, who should have been driving, was not in the vehicle. Chuck's partner, Sandy, stepped out slowly. Sandy's pursed lips and ashen face spoke volumes. Faith waited by the front door, her hands clasped tightly, to counter the fact that her mind was already reeling. "Love never fails." A compelling story. (Printed book: $12.99; PDF eBook: $9.99; both together, $19.99, direct from publisher; eBook reader versions available at *www.Amazon.com*; *www.BN.com*; *www.eChristian.com*.)

Worth the Cost?, by Jack Tsai, MD – The author was happily on his way to obtaining the American Dream until he decided to take seriously Jesus' command to "Come, follow me." Join him as he explores the cost of medical education and Christian discipleship. Planning to serve God in your future vocation? Take care  that your desires do not get side-tracked by the false promises of this world. Learn what you should be doing now so when you are done with your training you will still want to serve God. (Printed book: $12.99, PDF eBook: $9.99; both together: $19.99, direct from publisher; eBook reader versions available at *www.Amazon.com*; *www.BN.com*; *www.eChristian.com*.)

HEALTHY LIFE PRESS DISTRIBUTION UPDATE

Most Healthy Life Press books are available worldwide online and through bookstores. Distribution is through a major Christian distribution company: *www.STL-distribution.com*. Bookstores may order directly from STL. Our ePublications are available through *www.Amazon.com* (Kindle), *www.BN.com* (Nook), and for all commercial readers through *www.eChristian.com*. Unless specifically noted on the site itself, resources ordered via *www.healthylifepress.com* receive free shipping.

Nature: God's Second Book – An Essential Link to Restoring Your Personal Health and Wellness: Body, Mind, and Spirit, by Elvy P. Rolle – An inspirational book that looks at nature across the seasons of nature and of life. It uses the biblical Emmaus Journey as an analogy for life's journey, and offers ideas for using nature appreciation and exploration to reduce life's stresses. The author shares her personal story of how she came to grips with this concept after three trips to the emergency room. (**Full-color printed book: $12.99, available direct from publisher with free shipping, or wherever books are sold**; PDF eBook $8.99; both together: $18.99, direct from publisher only; eBook reader versions available at *www.Amazon.com; www.BN.com; www.eChristian.com.*)

ABOUT HEALTHY LIFE PRESS

Healthy Life Press was founded with a primary goal of helping previously unpublished authors to get their works to market, and to reissue worthy, previously published works that were no longer available. Our mission is to help people toward optimal vitality by providing resources promoting physical, emotional, spiritual, and relational health as viewed from a Christian perspective. We see health as a verb, and achieving optimal health as a process—a crucial process for followers of Christ if we are to love the Lord with all our heart, soul, mind, AND strength, and our neighbors as ourselves—for as long as He leaves us here. We are a collaborative and cooperative small Christian publisher.

For information about
publishing with us, e-mail:
healthylifepress@aol.com.

Recommended Resources – Books

 **52 Ways to Feel Great Today**, by David B. Biebel, DMin, James E. Dill, MD, and Bobbie Dill, RN – **Increase Your Vitality, Improve your Outlook.** Simple, fun, inexpensive things you can do to increase your vitality and improve your outlook. Why live an "ordinary" life when you could be experiencing the extraordinary? Don't settle for good enough when "great" is such a short stretch further. Make today great! (Printed book: $14.99.)

New Light on Depression, a CBA Gold Medallion winner, by David B. Biebel, DMin, and Harold Koenig, MD – The most exhaustive Christian resource on a subject that is more common than we might wish. Hope for those with depression and help for those who love them. (Printed book: $15.00.)

 **Your Mind at Its Best – 40 Ways To Keep Your Brain Sharp**, by David B. Biebel, DMin; James E. Dill, MD; and, Bobbie Dill, RN – Everyone wants their mind to function at high levels throughout life. In 40 easy-to-understand chapters, readers will discover a wide variety of tips and tricks to keep their minds sharp. Synthesizing science and self-help, Your Mind at Its Best makes fascinating neurological discoveries understandable and immediately applicable to readers of any age. (Printed book: $13.99.)

The A to Z Guide to Healthier Living, by David B. Biebel, DMin; James E. Dill, MD, and Bobbie Dill, RN – Discover the top changes an individual can make in order to achieve optimal health. MSRP: $12.99; Sale: 8.99, while supplies last: *www.healthylifepress.com.*

How to Help a Heartbroken Friend, by David B. Biebel, DMin – Helpful insights and guidelines for anyone who cares about those who are heartbroken and yet feel helpless in the face of the grieving. Learning to love quietly and share the burden as much as possible is a hard task, yet these thoughtful suggestions are bound to help one become an effective comforter. (Paperback: $10.00.)

RECOMMENDED RESOURCES
PRO-LIFE DVD SERIES

SEE *www.healthylifepress.com* (SELECT "DVD")

Window To the Womb (Pregnancy Care & Counseling Version) – Facts about fetal development, abortion complications, post-abortion syndrome, and healing. Separate chapters allow selection of specialized presentations to accommodate the needs and time constraints of their situations. (List Price: $34.95; Sale Price: $24.95.)

Eyewitness 2 (Public School Version) – This DVD has been used in many public schools. It is a fascinating journey through 38 weeks of pregnancy, showing developing babies via cutting edge digital ultrasound technology. Separate chapters allow viewing distinct segments individually. (List Price: $34.95; Sale Price: $24.95.)

COMBINATION Offer: Eyewitness 2 and Window to the Womb 2 (List Price: $84.90; Sale Price: $49.95.)

Window To The Womb (2 DVD Disc Set) Disc 1: Ian Donald (1910-1987) "A Prophetic Legacy;" Disc 2: "A Journey from Death To Life" (50 min) – Includes history of sonography and its increasing impact against abortion—more than 80% of expectant parents who "see" their developing baby choose for life. Perfect for counseling and education in Pregnancy Centers, Christian schools, home-schools, and churches. (List: $49.95; Sale: $34.95.)